Author's Purpose

Cause and Effect

Classify and Categorize

Compare and Contrast

Details and Facts

Draw Conclusions

Graphic Sources

Literary Elements

Main Idea and Details

Realism and Fantasy

Sequence

Steps in a Process

PICTURE IT!

A Comprehension Handbook

Author's Purpose

Inform

Entertain

Cause and Effect

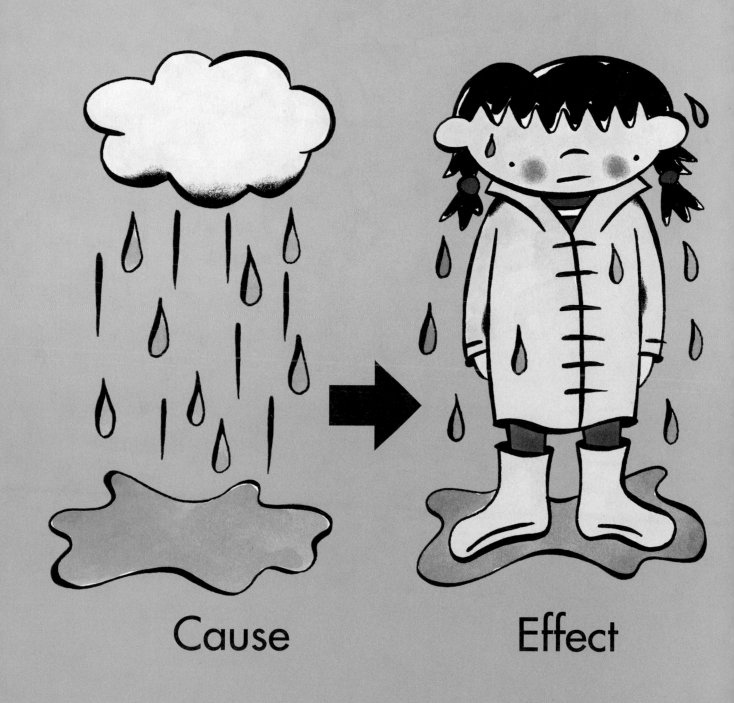

Cause

Effect

Classify and Categorize

Cars

Balls

Compare and Contrast

Details and Facts

Draw Conclusions

= Sad

Graphic Sources

eye

wing

beak

tail
feathers

Diagram

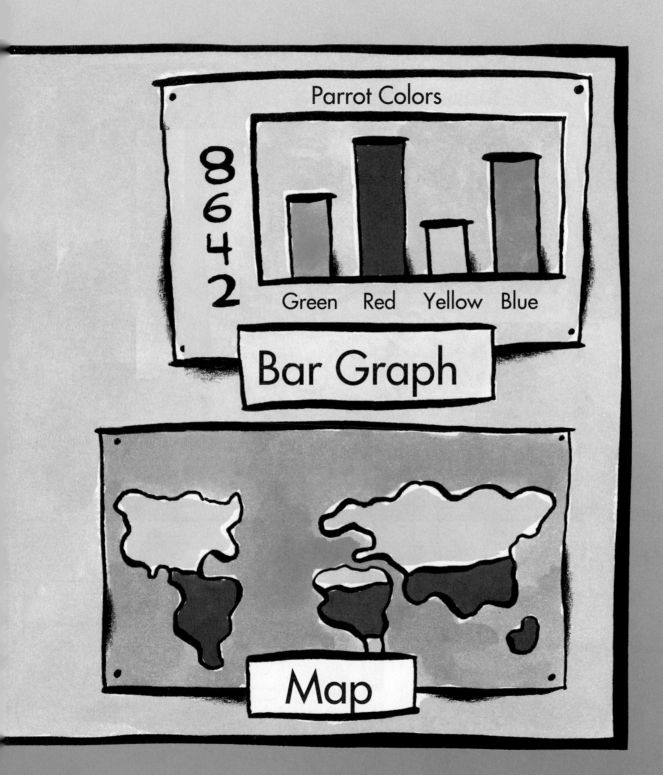

Literary Elements

Characters

BROTHER

MOMMY

DADDY

THE WOLF

SISTER

Setting

Plot

Beginning

Middle

End

Main Idea and Details

Main Idea

Details

Realism and Fantasy

Realism

Fantasy

Sequence

Steps in a Process

1

2

3

ISBN-13:   978-0-328-63434-7
ISBN-10:   0-328-63434-4
9 10 11 12 V011 17 16 15 14

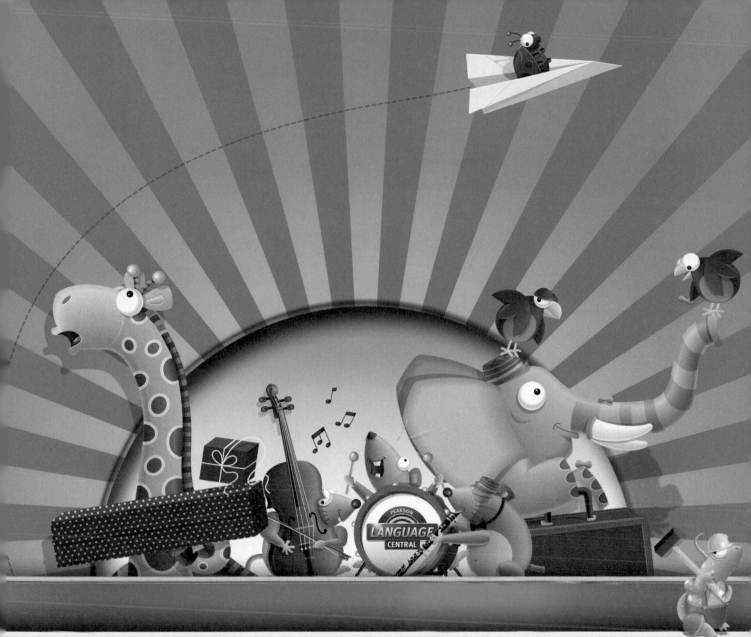

PEARSON LANGUAGE CENTRAL

ELD

Consulting Authors

Jim Cummins, Ph.D.

Lily Wong Fillmore, Ph.D.

Georgia García, Ph.D.

Jill Kerper Mora, Ed.D.

Glenview, Illinois • Boston, Massachusetts • Chandler, Arizona •
Upper Saddle River, New Jersey

Get Online

Picture It! A Comprehension Handbook PI•1–PI•15

Unit 1 Animals, Tame and Wild

Unit 2 People in Communities

Unit 3 Growing and Changing

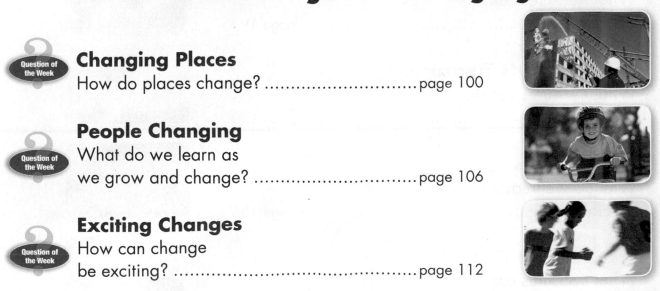

Contents

Grade 1 Contents

Unit 4 Surprising Treasures

Animals, Tame and Wild

How are people and animals important to one another?

Animal Needs
What do pets need?

Helping Animals
Who helps animals?

Animals That Help
How do animals help people?

Helping Wild Animals
How can we help wild animals?

Animals in Our Neighborhood
Which wild animals live in our neighborhood?

Watching Animals
What can we learn by watching wild animals?

Animals, Tame and Wild

cat

kitten

slept

come
drank
my
pet

What do pets need?

Pets need a place to live.
Pets need food and water.
Pets also need love.

Read the passage together.
Then circle the vocabulary words.

Sunny

Sam's dad had just (come) home.

He had a pet kitten for Sam!

Sam put out some cat toys and food.

The kitten drank some water and played.

Then she slept in the sun.

Sam said, "I will name my cat Sunny!"

· ·

Talk About It Complete the
sentence below.

> Sam put out _____ for his pet.
> *food, toys*

· ·

Your Turn What do pets need?
Tell a partner.

25

Literary Analysis We use special words to talk about when stories happen. The words *now* and *long ago* tell when stories happen.

Story 1

now

Story 2

long ago

- -

Talk About It Tell when the stories happen.

Story 1 happens _____.

Story 2 happens _____.

- -

Your Turn Look at the picture. Tell when the story happens.

Character and Setting Stories have people and animals in them. Some stories happen now. Other stories happen long ago.

Anna and Kate were happy to get a puppy. Spot liked his new home.

. . . .

Talk About It What is the story above about? When and where does the story happen?

> The characters are _____,
> _____, and _____.
>
> The story happens _____.

. . . .

Your Turn Look at the story on page 25. Where does the story happen? Tell a partner.

Sentences Some **sentences** tell what a person or thing does. The first word of a sentence needs a capital letter. Most sentences end with a period.

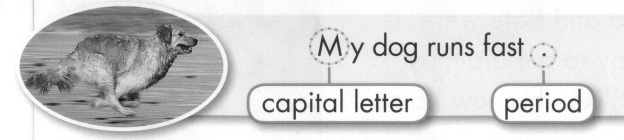

My dog runs fast .

capital letter   period

The fish swims .

capital letter   period

Talk About It Look at the sentence below. What is missing? Write it in.

The puppy drinks water

Your Turn Circle the letter that should be a capital.

the cat sleeps in the sun.

28

Animal Needs

Think about all of the things that are around you at home. What do you see in the picture?

. . . .

Talk About It Look at the words on page 24. Tell about each word.

. . . .

Produce Language Fill in the web below. Then write a sentence or draw a picture in your Weekly Concept Journal.

Pets Need

Vocabulary

examined

sick

vet

and
medicine
take
want

Who helps animals?

Pets can get sick. When pets get sick we take them to an animal doctor. This doctor is called a vet.

Read the passage together.
Then circle the vocabulary words.

The Vet

My cat Minny got (sick).

We had to take her to the vet.

The vet examined Minny.

Then the vet gave her medicine to feel better.

I want to be a vet and help animals.

Talk About It Complete the
sentences below.

Minny was _____.
sick, taken to the vet

The vet _____ Minny.
examined, gave medicine to

Your Turn How do vets help
animals? Tell a partner.

Comparing and Contrasting When two things are the same, they are alike. When two things are not the same, they are different.

These animals are **alike.**

These animals are **different.**

Talk About It Tell about the pictures above.

The kittens are alike because _____.

The dog and kitten are different because _____.

Your Turn Look at the horses. Tell how they are alike and different.

Compare/Contrast Character, Plot, Setting

When we read stories, we can compare the characters, what happens, and when the stories happen.

Story 1	Story 2
Tina's cat was sick. She took her cat to the vet.	Juan's dog was sick. He took his dog to the vet.

Talk About It Tell how these two stories are alike and different.

> The stories are alike because _____.
>
> The stories are different because _____.

Your Turn Read the story on page 31. How is it like the stories above? How is it different? Tell a partner.

Subjects of Sentences The **subject of a sentence** tells who or what the sentence is about.

(The vet) helps turtles.

(The bunny) eats grass.

(The lady) takes her cat to the vet.

Talk About It What is the subject of each sentence below?

The puppies drink water.   My cat plays with a toy.

Your Turn Complete the sentence. Use the word *dog* as the subject of the sentence.

The _____ went to the vet.

Helping Animals

Think about how people help animals. What is happening in the picture?

Talk About It Look at the words on page 30. Tell about each word.

Produce Language Draw a picture below. Show a vet helping an animal. Then write or draw in your Weekly Concept Journal.

PICTURE IT!

hiker

PICTURE IT!

woods

follow
help
lost
rescue
scent
use

How do animals help people?

Animals help people in many ways. Some animals, such as dogs, help find people who are lost or in danger.

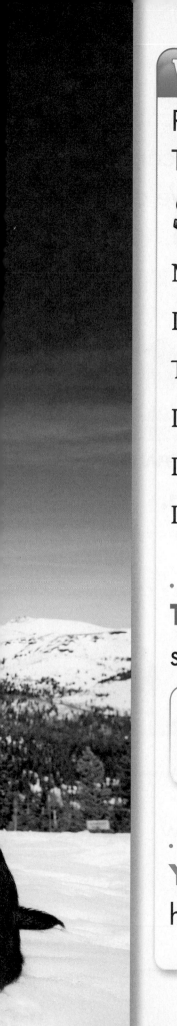

Read the passage together.
Then circle the vocabulary words.

Socks to the Rescue!

My name is Socks. I am a (rescue) dog.

I am a dog that can help find people.

Today a hiker is lost in the woods.

I help find the hiker.

I use my nose to follow the hiker's scent.

I lead the rescue team to the hiker.

Talk About It Complete the sentence below.

> Socks is a _____.
> *dog that helps people, rescue dog*

Your Turn How do rescue dogs help people? Tell a partner.

Describing We use special words to describe animals that are real or make-believe. We can use words to tell what the animal is like. We can use words to tell what the animal looks like.

The dog is **smart.**
The dog is **helpful.**

The dog is **brown.**
The dog is **big.**

Talk About It Look at the picture. Use words to tell what the rescue dog is like.

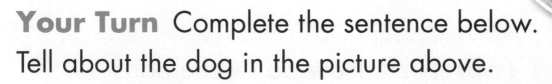

The rescue dog is _____.

Your Turn Complete the sentence below. Tell about the dog in the picture above.

The dog is _____.

Character and Setting Some stories have people and animals in them. Stories can happen in different places.

Sara fell off a horse in the woods. Sara hurt her leg. The horse made noise to help Sara. People heard the horse. They came to rescue Sara.

Talk About It Tell a partner about the story.

> The characters are _____ and _____.
>
> The story happens _____.

Your Turn Read the story on page 37. Where does the story happen? Tell a partner.

Predicates of Sentences A sentence names someone or something. Then it tells something about the person or thing. The **predicate of a sentence** tells something about the person or thing.

The dog **helps his owner.**

The horse **takes people places.**

Talk About It What is the predicate of each sentence below?

The dog loves her owner.

The dog helps people feel better.

Your Turn Circle the predicate of the sentence.

The dog went into the woods.

Animals That Help Think about how animals help people. What is happening in the picture below?

Talk About It Look at the words on page 36. Tell about each word.

Produce Language Draw a picture below. Show a dog helping a person. Then write or draw in your Weekly Concept Journal.

Vocabulary

PICTURE IT!

boats

PICTURE IT!

dolphins

PICTURE IT!

whales

clean
ocean
protect
safe
this

How can we help wild animals?

People can protect wild animals so they are not hurt. We can help keep the homes of wild animals safe.

Read the passage together.
Then circle the vocabulary words.

Whales and Dolphins

(Whales) and dolphins live in the ocean.

They need clean water to live.

Sometimes boats make ocean water dirty.

But we can help keep the water clean.

This can help protect whales and dolphins.

We can make whales and dolphins safe.

- -

Talk About It Complete the
sentence below.

_____ live in the ocean.
Whales, Dolphins

- -

Your Turn How do people help whales
and dolphins? Tell a partner.

Retelling We use words to tell about things that happened. When we tell about things that already happened, we change the word *is* to *was*.

Now	Already Happened

The girl **is eating**.	The girl **was eating**.

Talk About It
Tell something that a friend is doing now. Then say a sentence that shows it already happened.

> My friend is _____.
>
> My friend was _____.

Your Turn Tell what the whale in the picture was doing.

The whale was _____.

Main Idea When we read, we can tell what happened and what a story is about.

People can help whales that end up on shore. People can help keep these whales wet. This way, people can help the whales stay alive.

Talk About It Look at the sentences above. What are they all about? Tell a partner.

Your Turn Look at the picture. What is it about? Tell what is happening.

Word Order The words in a sentence go in a certain order. With **word order,** we name someone or something. Then we tell about the person or the thing.

Name	Then Tell More
Whales	live in the ocean.
The dolphin	jumped in the water.

Talk About It Put the words below together to make a sentence. Say the words in the correct order.

live in the ocean	whales
dolphins	are big animals

Your Turn Say a sentence about dolphins or whales. Put the words in the correct order.

Helping Wild Animals Look at the picture below. How do you think people help dolphins?

Talk About It Look at the words on page 42. Tell about each word.

Produce Language Draw a picture below. Show people helping wild animals. Then write or draw in your Weekly Concept Journal.

Vocabulary

PICTURE IT!

flying

PICTURE IT!

nest

branches
eggs
tree

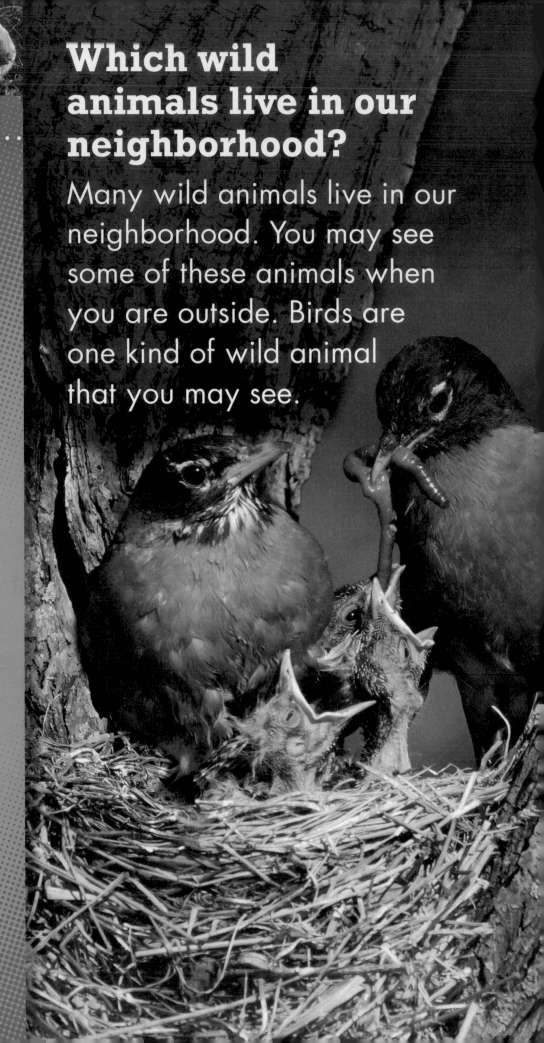

Which wild animals live in our neighborhood?

Many wild animals live in our neighborhood. You may see some of these animals when you are outside. Birds are one kind of wild animal that you may see.

Read the passage together.
Then circle the vocabulary words.

Bird Watching

Birds are all around your neighborhood.

You may see birds (flying) in the sky.

You may also hear birds singing.

You may see a bird make its nest too.
Nests are high up on tree branches.

Nests keep baby bird eggs safe.

Talk About It Complete the sentence below.

> You may see birds _____.
> *flying, making nests*

Your Turn What can you see birds doing? Tell a partner.

Retelling We use words to tell about things that have happened. We use the word *and* to tell about more than one thing.

The bird **was sitting.**
The bird **was singing.**
The bird **was sitting and singing.**

· ·

Talk About It Look at the picture.
Tell what the bird was doing.

The bird was _____.

The bird was _____.

The bird was _____ and _____.

· ·

Your Turn Tell two things that you were doing earlier today.

I was _____ and _____.

Main Idea When we read stories and sentences, we can tell what they are about in our own words.

Birds make nests.

Birds use twigs and grass to make a nest.

The nest is very important.

Talk About It What are the sentences all about? Tell a partner.

Birds _____ .

Your Turn Read the story on page 49. What are the sentences all about? Use the word *and* in your sentence.

Statements A **statement** is a sentence that names someone or something. It tells about the person or the thing. The first word of a statement needs a capital letter. Statements end with a period.

(B)aby birds hatch from eggs.

capital letter   period

. . . .

Talk About It Look at the statements below. What is missing? Write it in.

The bird is near a flower

The bird flies from tree to tree

. . . .

Your Turn Circle the letters that should be capital letters.

the bird was hungry.

four baby birds hatched.

Animals in Our Neighborhood Think about the wild animals that live in a neighborhood. What do you see in the picture below?

Talk About It Look at the words on page 48. Tell about each word.

Produce Language Draw a picture below. Show wild animals in your neighborhood. Then write words or draw pictures in your Weekly Concept Journal.

Vocabulary

elephant

herd

leads
many
scientists
study

What can we learn by watching wild animals?

We learn about animals by watching them. We can learn what they eat. We can also learn how animals, such as elephants, care for their babies.

Read the passage together.
Then circle the vocabulary words.

African Elephants

Some (scientists) study animals in Africa.

They watch elephant families to learn.

Many families live together in a herd.

All mothers in the herd protect the calves.

The oldest mother elephant leads the herd.

She helps the herd find food and water.

· ·

Talk About It Complete the sentence below.

> Scientists have learned that _____.
> *elephant families live together in a herd, the oldest mother leads the herd*

· ·

Your Turn What have people learned by watching elephants? Tell a partner.

Cause and Effect Relationship

We use words to tell what happened and why it happened. The word *because* tells why things happened.

The tiger was tired.   The tiger yawned.

The tiger yawned **because** the tiger was tired.

Talk About It Look at the pictures above. Tell what happened and why it happened.

> The tiger _____ because _____ .

Your Turn Look at the picture. Tell why the elephant is eating.

> The elephant is eating because _____ .

Cause and Effect As you read, think about things that happen and why those things happen. Look for clue words, such as *because*, to tell why things happen.

The zebras drank water because they were thirsty.

Talk About It What happened? Why did it happen?

The zebras _____. They were _____.

Your Turn What is happening in this picture? Why is it happening? Tell a partner.

The giraffes _____ because _____.

Questions A **question** is a sentence that asks who, what, when, where, why, or how. Questions begin with a capital letter and end with a question mark.

What are the hippos doing?

capital   question mark

Talk About It Look at the question below. What is missing? Write it in.

What does this bird eat

Your Turn Say a question you can ask about the picture.

58

Watching Animals Think about what people learn by watching wild animals. Think about what you learned about elephants and other wild animals. What do you see in the picture below?

Talk About It Look at the words on page 54. Tell about each word.

Produce Language Draw a picture below. Show what you would see if you were watching a wild animal. Then write words or draw in your Weekly Concept Journal.

Get Online!

Hear it!
See it!
Do it!

- Big Question Video
- Concept Talk Video
- Envision It! Animation
- Grammar Jammer
- Daily Journal

People in Communities

THE BIG ?

What is a community?

Families
What does a family do together?

At School
How is a school a community?

Community Workers
Who works to make our community a nice place?

Animal Communities
How do animal communities work together
to survive?

Plant and Animal Communities
How are plant and animal communities important
to each other?

Insect Communities
How is an insect community like a community
of people?

People in Communities

Vocabulary

family

meal

gather
good
think
wash

What does a family do together?

A family is a community. A family works and plays together. The people in a family help each other too.

Read the passage together.
Then circle the vocabulary words.

A Family

People in a (family) want to help one another.

They help cook food and wash clothes.

Many families think it is good to be together.

They gather to eat a meal.

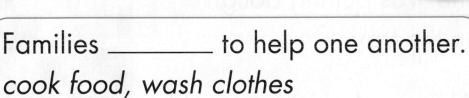

They gather to play a game.

Talk About It Complete
the sentences below.

Families _____ to help one another.
cook food, wash clothes

Families like to gather _____.
for a meal, to play a game

Your Turn What can a family
do together? Tell a partner.

63

Retelling We use words to tell about things that happened. Use *was* and *were* with action words that end in *-ing*.

were + helping	We **were helping** Dad wash the dog.
was + shaking	The dog **was shaking** itself dry.

· ·

Talk About It Circle the words that tell about things that happened.

> She was putting dough on the tray.
>
> We were baking a snack.

· ·

Your Turn Tell a partner something you were doing today. Use an *-ing* word in your sentence.

I was _____.

Main Idea and Details

The **main idea** is the big idea in a story or picture. **Details** tell about the main idea.

Main Idea	Details
Carmen and her mom were making tacos.	They were using meat. They were using cheese.

. . . .

Talk About It Look at the picture above. What is the main idea? What are the details?

. . . .

Your Turn Look at the picture. Circle the main idea. Tell a partner one detail.

The child was playing a game.

The child was washing dishes.

Nouns Words that name people, places, and things are **nouns.** Some nouns are circled in the sentences below.

Sentences

(Roberta) has a (family).

A (family) lives in the (house).

The (boy) cooked the (meal).

Talk About It Circle the nouns below.

The girl was playing a game.

The family lives in the house.

Your Turn Look at the picture. Use nouns to name what you see.

Think, Talk, and Write

Families A family is a community. Tell a partner what families can do together.

have fun

help each other

Talk About It Review the words on page 62. Show a partner what each word means.

Produce Language Write about something a family can do together. First draw a picture. Complete the sentences. Then write in your Weekly Concept Journal.

Families can do many things _____.

Families _____ together.

Vocabulary

janitor

nurse

be
make
principal

How is a school a community?

Many people work together in a school. Some people teach. Other people clean or run the school. Children learn at the school.

Read the passage together.
Then circle the vocabulary words.

School Workers

Teachers help children learn.

A (nurse) helps children who may be sick.

Lunch workers make and serve food.

A janitor keeps the school clean.

The principal runs the school.

· ·

Talk About It Complete the sentences below.

> A janitor _____.
> *is a school worker, cleans the school*
>
> Lunch workers _____.
> *make food, serve food to the children*

· ·

Your Turn Who works
in a school? Tell a partner.

Cause-and-Effect Relationship

We use words to tell what happens and why. The word *because* helps us tell why.

The girl went to the nurse **because** she felt sick.

Talk About It Look at the picture above. What happened and why?

_____ because _____ .

Your Turn Look at the picture. Tell why the janitor is cleaning the floor.

The janitor is cleaning the floor because _____ .

FORM & FUNCTION

Cause and Effect A thing that happens is an **effect.** Why a thing happens is a **cause.** You can use the word *because* to tell a cause.

What Happened	**Why It Happened**
⬇	⬇

The children sit on the floor **because** it is story time.

Talk About It Look at the picture. Tell why the boy raises his hand.

> The boy raises his hand because _____.

Your Turn Look at this picture. Tell what the girl does when she gets her lunch.

_____ because she has her lunch.

71

Proper Nouns We use **proper nouns** to name special people, places, and things. Proper nouns begin with a capital letter, such as *A* or *B*.

Dr. Jones

Washington School

Pacific Ocean

Talk About It Circle the proper nouns in the sentences.

That bell is the Liberty Bell.

The San Gabriel River is a long river.

Your Turn Match the proper nouns to the pictures.

Ms. Gomez

California

Think, Talk, and Write

students and teacher

school worker

At School Think about the people who are part of the school community. Tell a partner how a school is a community.

Talk About It Review the words on page 68. Tell or show a partner what each word means.

Produce Language Write about people in your school community. First draw a picture. Complete the sentences. Then write in your Weekly Concept Journal.

My school is a _____.

_____ is part of the school community.

Vocabulary

PICTURE IT!

litter

PICTURE IT!

people

PICTURE IT!

playground

fixed

nice

Who works to make our community a nice place?

A community is a nice place when people take care of it. People need to clean up. People need to fix things that are broken.

Read the passage together.
Then circle the vocabulary words.

Community Park

The park has not always been a (nice) place.

People in the community wanted to help.

So they picked up litter in the park.

They also fixed the playground.

Now the park is a nice place to be!

· ·

Talk About It Complete the
sentence below.

People in the community helped
by _____.
picking up litter, fixing the playground

· ·

Your Turn Who helped make the
park a nice place? Tell a partner.

Asking Questions We ask questions when we want to know something. Some questions start with *What are* or *What is.*

Question	Answer
What are the girls doing?	The girls are cleaning up a park.
What is the girl picking up?	The girl is picking up litter.

Talk About It Circle the words *What are* and *What is* in the questions below.

> What is a community?
>
> What are the people fixing?

Your Turn Look at the picture. What question can you ask about it? Tell a partner.

What _____?

Author's Purpose An **author's purpose** tells why an author writes something. We can ask a question to help us understand an author's purpose.

Make the park a nice place.

Help us clean it up!

What is the author of the sign trying to tell us?

- -

Talk About It Look at the sign above. Tell why you think the author wrote it.

> The author wrote the sign because _____.

- -

Your Turn Look at the story "Community Park" on page 75. What is the author trying to tell us? Tell a partner.

Special Titles We use **special titles** to tell who people are or what they do. Special titles start with capital letters.

Doctor
Gonzalez

Principal
Boyd

Ms.
Young

Talk About It Circle the titles below.

Mr. Williams

Judge Santoro

Your Turn Write a title in front of each name. Start each title with a capital letter.

_____ Tully

_____ Foley

Community Workers

Tell a partner about the different people who work to make your community a nice place.

police officers

trash collector

Talk About It Review the words on page 74. Tell or show a partner what each word means.

Produce Language Write about a person who helps make your community a nice place. First draw a picture. Complete the sentences. Then write in your Weekly Concept Journal.

_____ makes our community a nice place.

_____ makes our community nice by _____ .

Vocabulary

ground

hole

meerkats

communities
inside
under

How do animal communities work together to survive?

Most people live together in communities. Some kinds of animals live in communities too. They help each other by doing different jobs.

Read the passage together.
Then circle the vocabulary words.

Meerkats

(Meerkats) live in communities.

They live inside a hole under the ground.

Some meerkats keep the hole clean.

Some meerkats take care of the babies.

Some meerkats watch out for danger.

. . . .

Talk About It Complete
the sentences below.

Meerkats live _____.
in holes, in communities

Some meerkats _____.
take care of babies, watch for danger

. . . .

Your Turn How do meerkats
help each other? Tell a partner.

81

Sequencing We use words to tell when things happen. Special words help us tell things in order.

First

Next

Last

First, you wake up.

Next, you eat breakfast.

Last, you go to school.

Talk About It Tell about what you do before you go to school.

First, I _____.

Next, I _____.

Last, I _____.

Your Turn What is something else you do in order? Tell a partner.

Sequence People and animals do things in order. **Sequence** is another word for order. When you read, look for words that tell order.

First, meerkats wake up.

Next, they look for food.

Last, they eat their meals.

Talk About It What do meerkats do first? What do they do next? What do they do last?

Your Turn These pictures of a chicken hatching from an egg are not in order. Tell what happens first, next, and last.

Proper Nouns **Proper nouns**

are the names of people, places, or important things. Proper nouns always begin with a capital letter.

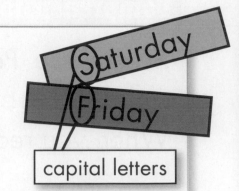

capital letters

Talk About It Days of the week are examples of proper nouns. Draw an X on the days of the week that you are in school.

Sunday	Monday	Tuesday	Wednesday	Thursday	Friday	Saturday

Your Turn Write the days of the week. Use capital letters at the start of each word.

_____   _____

_____   _____

_____   _____

_____

Think, Talk, and Write

penguins

elephants

Animal Communities

Meerkats live in communities. Other animals live in communities too. How does this help them survive? Tell a partner.

. . . .

Talk About It Review the words on page 80. Tell or show a partner what each word means.

. . . .

Produce Language Write about an animal that lives in a community. First draw a picture of the animal you choose. Complete the sentences. Then write in your Weekly Concept Journal.

_____ live in communities.

They help each other _____.

Plant and Animal Communities

Vocabulary

chain

food

grass

strong
these

How are plant and animal communities important to each other?

Animals and plants live together in communities. They give each other food. They share places to live.

Read the passage together.
Then circle the vocabulary words.

Food Chain

(Grass) grows out of the ground.

Grass is food for cows.

Cows use the grass to grow strong.

These cows give us milk to drink.

This is called a food chain.

Talk About It Complete
the sentence below.

Grass _____ .

*grows out of the ground,
is food for cows*

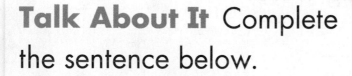

Your Turn Why is grass important
to cows? Tell a partner.

Describing We can use words to tell about people, places, and things.

The cow
is **brown.**

The bird
is **white.**

The grass
is **green.**

Talk About It Complete each sentence.
Use a describing word.

Milk is _____.

The cow is _____.

Your Turn Complete the sentence.

The cow is _____.

Author's Purpose The **author's purpose** tells why a person wrote something. Sometimes the author's purpose is to teach us.

This book can teach us about plants and animals. This is the **author's purpose.**

Plants and Animals

Talk About It Tell why the author wrote the book above.

The author's purpose is _____.

Your Turn Look at the story "Food Chain" on page 87. What did the author want to teach us? Tell a partner.

Singular and Plural Nouns A **singular noun** names one person, place, or thing. A **plural noun** names more than one. Many plural nouns end in *-s*.

Singular Nouns	Plural Nouns
cow	cows
tree	trees
nest	nests

Talk About It Complete each sentence. Use a singular noun.

> The _____ eats grass.
>
> The _____ is in a tree.

Your Turn Complete the sentences below. Circle the correct noun.

The *nest, nests* is in the tree.

The *bird, birds* build a nest.

Think, Talk, and Write

Plant and Animal Communities Tell a partner how plant and animal communities are important to each other.

food

shelter

Talk About It Review the words on page 86. Show a partner what each word means.

Produce Language Write about how plants and animals are important to each other. First draw a picture. Complete the sentences. Then write in your Weekly Concept Journal.

Plants and animals are important to each other because _____.

Animals need plants to _____.

PICTURE IT!

bees

PICTURE IT!

hive

PICTURE IT!

queen

**insects
return
some**

How is an insect community like a community of people?

Insects live together like people do. They get food for each other. They make homes where all of the insects can live.

Read the passage together.
Then circle the vocabulary words.

BEES

(Bees) are insects.

They live in a hive.

Some bees leave the hive every day.

They return with food for the hive.

The queen bee lays eggs in the hive.

Talk About It Complete
the sentence below.

Bees _____.
are insects, live in a hive

Your Turn How is a hive
a community? Tell a partner.

93

Comparing We can use words to tell how things are alike and different.

fly

bee

Alike	Different
A fly has wings. A bee has wings.	A fly is black. A bee is yellow.
The insects both have wings.	The insects have different colors.

Talk About It Look at the pictures. How are the insects alike?

The insects both _____.

Your Turn Look at the pictures above. Tell what is different.

The insects have different _____.

Compare and Contrast We **compare** when we tell how things are alike. We **contrast** when things are different.

Compare = Alike	Contrast = Different
The hive is busy. The town is busy.	The hive has bees. The town has people.

Talk About It Look at the pictures above. Tell how the hive and town are alike. Tell how the hive and town are different.

Your Turn Tell one way a bee and a person are alike and different.

Nouns in Sentences A **noun** names a person, place, or thing. A noun can come at the beginning of a sentence. It can also come at the end of a sentence.

The **bee** flies.

The **picture** is of **bees.**

Talk About It Circle the nouns in the sentences.

The bees live in the hive.

The hive is in a tree.

Your Turn Complete each sentence with a noun.

Many _____ live in the hive.

The _____ is on the leaf.

Insect Communities Think about how bees are like people. Tell a partner how an insect community is like a community of people.

special jobs

work together

Talk About It Review the words on page 92. Tell or show a partner what each word means.

Produce Language Write about how people and insect communities are the same. First draw a picture. Complete the sentences. Then write in your Weekly Concept Journal.

Insect and people communities are _____ .

Both people and insects _____ .

Get Online!

Hear it!
See it!
Do it!

- Big Question Video
- Concept Talk Video
- Envision It! Animation
- Grammar Jammer
- Daily Journal

Growing and Changing

 What is changing in our world?

Changing Places
How do places change?

People Changing
What do we learn as we grow and change?

Exciting Changes
How can change be exciting?

Weather Changes
How does weather change?

The Seasons
What happens as the seasons change?

Animal Changes
What do animals do when the seasons change?

Growing and Changing

Vocabulary

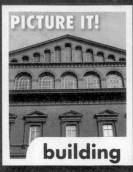

building

land

**always
stands
things
torn**

How do places change?

A building is a place where people live and work. Sometimes a building can change. So can the land a building stands on.

Read the passage together.
Then circle the vocabulary words.

A New Place

(Things) don't always stay the same.

Sometimes a building can get old.

The building may be torn down.

Sometimes a new building is made.

Trees and flowers may grow on the land.

Animals may also come live on the land.

Talk About It Complete
the sentence below.

A building _____.
can get old, may be torn down

Your Turn How can land change?
Tell a partner.

Sequencing We use words to tell when things happen. Special words help us tell things in order.

At first   Now

At first, there was only grass on the land.

Now, there are houses on the land.

Talk About It Tell about how your home has changed.

At first, my home _____.

Now, my home _____.

Your Turn How has your family changed? Tell a partner.

At first, _____. Now, _____.

Sequence We read about things done in a certain order. Words such as *at first* and *now* tell about order.

At first, the building was torn down.

Now, flowers and grass grow there.

Talk About It Look at the pictures above. What happens at first? What happens now?

Your Turn Look at these pictures of the forest. Tell what happens at first. Tell what happens now.

Action Verbs A verb that shows how someone does something is called an **action verb.**

I **run** in the grass.

Flowers **grow** on the land.

Talk About It Tell your partner the action verb in each sentence.

We look at the old building.

They built a new building.

Your Turn Write a sentence with one of these action words: *grow, run.*

_____

_____

Think, Talk, and Write

Changing Places Think about how places change. Tell a partner how a place in your home, school, or neighborhood has changed.

at first

now

Talk About It Review the words on page 100. Tell or show a partner what each word means.

Produce Language Write about how your home, school, or neighborhood has changed. First draw a picture of the place. Complete the sentences. Then write in your Weekly Concept Journal.

_____ has changed.

At first, _____.

Now, _____.

Vocabulary

PICTURE IT!

bicycle

PICTURE IT!

wheels

continue
every
riding
sure

What do we learn as we grow and change?

Everyone changes as they grow. As we grow, we learn to do new things. One of the things we may learn to do is ride a bicycle.

Read the passage together.
Then circle the vocabulary words.

The Bicycle

Miguel's new (bicycle) had two wheels.

Every day he tried riding it.

Sometimes he fell off.

But Miguel wanted to continue riding.

He was sure he could do it.

He learned to ride his bicycle!

Talk About It Complete the sentence.

Miguel's bicycle _____.
was new, had two wheels

Your Turn What did Miguel learn? Tell a partner.

107

Describing We use action
words to tell more about what happens.

David **rode** his
new bicycle.

Sasha **walked**
to school.

Talk About It Tell about something
you did yesterday. Use an action word.

Yesterday, I _____.

Your Turn Tell about something
you have learned to do.

Plot What happens in a story is called the **plot.**

Nadia did not know how to speak much English. Her teacher taught her some words. Nadia practiced. Soon she could talk to her friends.

Talk About It What is the plot of the story above? Tell a partner.

Your Turn Think about a story you know. Write the plot.

_____

_____

Verbs That Add -s A **verb** is a word that shows action.

I	walk
You	walk
They	walk

He	walk**s**
She	walk**s**
It	walk**s**

Some verbs don't have an *-s*.
Some verbs have an *-s* at the end.

Talk About It Circle the correct verb in each sentence.

She *play, plays* baseball.

I *run, runs* very fast.

He *learn, learns* how to swim.

Your Turn Write a verb with *-s*.

He _____ a bicycle.

She _____ to school.

Think, Talk, and Write

swim

tie shoes

People Changing Think about how Miguel learned to ride a bicycle. Tell a partner about something new that you have learned to do as you have grown.

Talk About It Review the words on page 106. Tell or show a partner what each word means.

Produce Language Write about something new that you have learned to do. First draw a picture of the new thing you learned how to do. Complete the sentences. Then write in your Weekly Concept Journal.

At first, I did not know how to _____.

When I grew, I learned to _____.

PICTURE IT!

house

PICTURE IT!

school

PICTURE IT!

soccer

friends
our
scared

How can change be exciting?

When things change in our lives, it can be scary. But those things can also be exciting. Meeting new friends is a change that can be exciting.

Read the passage together.
Then circle the vocabulary words.

The Soccer Team

Jill was (scared) to move to a new house.

She also had to go to a new school.

After Jill moved, she joined a soccer team.

There, Jill made some new friends!

Talk About It Complete the sentences.

Jill was scared because _____.
*she had to move to a new house,
she had to go to a new school*

After Jill moved, _____.
*she joined a soccer team, she met
some new friends*

Your Turn Why was moving scary
and exciting for Jill? Tell a partner.

Defining We use words to tell about kinds of things. A school and house are alike. They are both buildings.

A house **is a building.**   A school **is a building.**

Talk About It Tell about each word.

Soccer is a _____.
(sport, building)

Baseball is a _____.
(friend, sport)

Your Turn Tell how the two things are alike.

    Soccer and baseball are _____.

Classify and Categorize

People put alike things in groups.

Things With Wheels	Things Without Wheels
car, wagon	house

Talk About It How are the things above alike? Tell a partner.

Your Turn Look at the pictures. Tell how the things below are alike.

soccer ball   baseball   basketball

Verbs That Do Not Add -s

A **verb** is a word that shows action. When there are two or more people or things in the subject, do not add -s to the verb in the predicate.

We **pack** our clothes.

Two people **put** boxes in the truck.

The boy and girl **move** to a new place.

- -

Talk About It Complete the sentences below.

> The students _____ soccer.
>
> We _____ soccer.

- -

Your Turn Write the correct verb.

We _____ to a new house.

(move, moves)

Think, Talk, and Write

something funny

Exciting Changes Changes can be exciting. Think about all of the changes that happened when Jill moved to a new house. Tell a partner about a change that is exciting.

something new

Talk About It Review the words on page 112. Tell or show a partner what each word means.

Produce Language Write about a change that was exciting. First draw a picture of the exciting change. Complete the sentences. Then write in your Weekly Concept Journal.

_____ was an exciting change.

It was exciting because _____.

Vocabulary

cloudy

rain

again
drops
soon
weather

How does weather change?

Weather changes every day. Sometimes there are clouds in the sky. Sometimes there are not. Sometimes the sun shines. Other times it might rain or snow.

Read the passage together.
Then circle the vocabulary words.

Rain

(Rain) comes from cloudy skies.

First, tiny drops of water form.

Next, the drops get heavy.

Soon, the rain falls from the clouds.

At last, the rain stops and the sun shines.

The weather is nice again.

Talk About It Complete the sentence.

Rain _____.

comes from clouds, is tiny drops of water

Your Turn How does rain start?
Tell a partner.

Sequencing We use words to tell when things happen. Special words help us tell things in order.

First — First, snow falls.

Next — Next, we play.

Last — Last, we make a snowman.

Talk About It What did you do today?
Tell a partner. Use *first*, *next*, and *last*.

First, I _____.

Next, I _____.

Last, I _____.

Your Turn What is something else you do in order? Tell a partner.

Sequence Things happen in order. When you read, certain words help tell order: *first, next,* and *last.*

First, the sun sets.

Next, the sky gets dark.

Last, we see the moon.

Talk About It Look at the pictures above. What happens first? What happens next? What happens last? Tell a partner.

Your Turn Look at the story "Rain" on page 119. What happens first? What happens next? What happens last?

Verbs for Present and for Past

Verbs can tell about what happens now.
Verbs can also tell about the past.

Present	Past
Now, she **plays** in the snow.	Yesterday, she **played** in the snow.
Now, she **jumps** in a puddle.	Last week, she **jumped** in a puddle.

. . . .

Talk About It Which verb tells what happens now? Which verb tells about the past?

The rain falls.

I walked in the rain.

. . . .

Your Turn Choose the correct verb.

Last night, it _____.

(*snows, snowed*)

Think, Talk, and Write

Weather Changes Weather changes every day. Think about what happens when it rains. Tell a partner how the weather changes around you.

sunny

cloudy

Talk About It Review the words on page 118. Tell or show a partner what each word means.

Produce Language Write about how the weather changes. First draw a picture of three different kinds of weather. Complete the sentences. Then write in your Weekly Concept Journal.

The weather can be _____.

The weather can change to _____.

Vocabulary

PICTURE IT!

birds

PICTURE IT!

bloom

push
spring
wait

What happens as the seasons change?

There are four seasons each year. They are summer, fall, winter, and spring. Many things happen during each season.

Read the passage together.
Then circle the vocabulary words.

Springtime

In winter, many people (wait) for spring.

Trees and flowers bloom in spring.

New plants push up through the ground.

Animals wake up from long winter naps.

Birds begin to sing and build nests.

．．．．．．．．．．．．．．．．．．．．．．．．．．．．．．．．．．．．

Talk About It Complete the sentences.

In spring, _____ .
trees and flowers bloom, plants push up through the ground

Birds begin to _____ .
sing, build nests

．．．．．．．．．．．．．．．．．．．．．．．．．．．．．．．．．．．．

Your Turn What changes happen in spring? Tell a partner.

Defining We use words to tell about other words. We put things into groups.

 A robin **is a bird.**    A blue jay **is a bird.**

A robin and a blue jay belong to the same group.

. . . .

Talk About It Tell about each picture. Which ones belong in the same group?

A fox is an animal.   A bear is an animal.   A daisy is a plant.

. . . .

Your Turn What else could you put in the same group as a daisy? Tell a partner.

A daisy and a _____ belong to the same group.

Classify and Categorize

People put like things in a group.

Things Seen in Spring	Things Not Seen in Spring
rain, flowers, leaves	snow

Talk About It Why is snow not in the same group as leaves? Tell a partner.

Your Turn Look at these pictures. Which things belong in the same group? Tell a partner why.

 **bird**

 **nest**

 **egg**

 **clouds**

Verbs A **verb** can tell about things that happen now or that happened in the past.

Now	Past
I **am** planting.	I **was** planting.
He **is** planting.	He **was** planting.
We **are** planting.	We **were** planting.

Talk About It Read these sentences. Which verb tells about now? Which tells about the past?

It is spring.

Yesterday, it was raining.

Your Turn Choose the correct verb.

Yesterday _____ sunny. *(is, was)*

Today the birds _____ singing. *(are, were)*

Think, Talk, and Write

The Seasons Think about what changes happen in spring. Tell a partner some changes that happen in other seasons.

fall

winter

Talk About It Review the words on page 124. Tell or show a partner what each word means.

Produce Language Write about what changes happen in a season. First draw a picture of the season you choose. Complete the sentence. Then write in your Weekly Concept Journal.

When _____ comes, there are changes.

Vocabulary

geese

sea turtle

before
migrate
south
won't

What do animals do when the seasons change?

Many things happen when the seasons change. Before winter, many animals build nests or dens. Some animals migrate to look for food.

Read the passage together.
Then circle the vocabulary words.

Animals Migrate

Some animals (migrate) before winter.

They migrate to warmer places.

Geese fly south. Whales swim south.

Animals such as the sea turtle go very far.

They find food so they won't be hungry.

· ·

Talk About It Complete the sentences.

_____ migrate south.
Geese, Whales, Sea turtles

Animals migrate _____.
to warmer places, to find food

· ·

Your Turn What do some animals do during winter? Tell a partner.

Sequencing We use words to tell the order that things happen. *Before* and *after* are words that help us tell things in order.

Autumn

Winter

Spring

Before winter, it is autumn.

After winter, it is spring.

. . . .

Talk About It What do you do before school? Tell a partner.

> Before school, I _____.

. . . .

Your Turn Tell about what you do after school ends in the summer.

Steps in a Process When we do something, we do it in order. These are **steps in a process.** Words such as *before* and *after* help tell the steps in a process.

Before winter, turtles migrate.
They swim to beaches.
They build nests. They lay eggs.
After winter, the eggs hatch.
The turtles go back to the sea.

Talk About It What do sea turtles do before winter? What do they do after winter?

Your Turn These pictures show geese. Tell about the two steps geese take when they migrate. Use the words *before* and *after*.

Contractions With *Not* A **contraction** is a shorter way to write two words. A special mark shows the missing letters.

Word + not	Contraction
are + not	**aren't**
can + not	**can't**
is + not	**isn't**
do + not	**don't**
have + not	**haven't**

Talk About It Circle the contractions.

Whales can't walk.

Whales aren't small.

Your Turn Complete the sentence. Use a contraction from above.

Dogs _____ migrate.

134

Think, Talk, and Write

Animal Changes Think about what geese, whales, and sea turtles do when winter comes. Tell a partner some things that animals do when the seasons change.

migrate

build nests

Talk About It Review the words on page 130. Tell or show a partner what each word means.

Produce Language Write about what some animals do in winter. First draw a picture of the animal you choose. Complete the sentences. Then write in your Weekly Concept Journal.

When winter comes, _____.

They do this because _____.

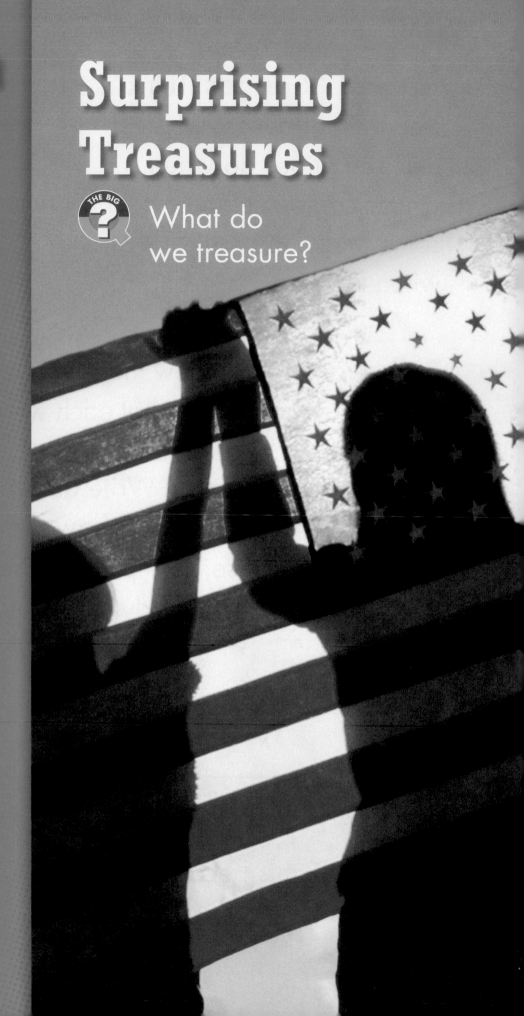

Get Online!

Hear it!
See it!
Do it!

- Big Question Video
- Concept Talk Video
- Envision It! Animation
- Grammar Jammer
- Daily Journal

Surprising Treasures

THE BIG ?

What do
we treasure?

Surprising Treasures
How can a surprise be a treasure?

Making Treasures
What treasures can we create?

Our Country's Treasures
What treasures can we find in our country?

Special Days
Why do we treasure special days?

Treasures at Home
What treasures can we share at home?

Our Sharing Treasures
What treasures can we share with neighbors?

Vocabulary

grandson

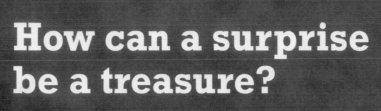

surprise

treasure
value
would

How can a surprise be a treasure?

A surprise is a gift that you don't expect. A treasure is something that has a lot of value. Sometimes a person can be a surprise and a treasure.

Read the passage together.
Then circle the vocabulary words.

The Surprise

"Close your eyes for a surprise," Mom said.

Juan wondered what the surprise would be.

"I would like a treasure," Juan said.

"This one has a lot of value," Mom said.

Juan looked up and saw his grandmother!

She had come to visit her grandson!

Talk About It Complete the sentence below.

> Juan _____.
> *did not know what to expect,
> saw his grandmother*

Your Turn Tell a partner how you would feel if you got a surprise visit.

Interpreting We use words to tell what we think about something.

I think that the boy is happy.

Talk About It Look at the picture. Tell what you think about the girl.

I think _____ .

Your Turn Look at the picture. Tell what you think.

Draw Conclusions When you read a story or look at pictures, you can **draw conclusions,** or figure out more about a character or story.

Example: I think this family is going on a trip.

Talk About It Look at this picture. Tell your partner your conclusion.

Your Turn Look at the story "The Surprise" on page 139. Draw a conclusion about how Juan feels at the end of the story.

I think _____ .

Adjectives Words that are used to describe people, places, or things are called **adjectives.**

tall person

big city

red ball

Talk About It Use an adjective to tell about the picture.

This is a _____ box.

Your Turn Tell about the balloon. Use adjectives.

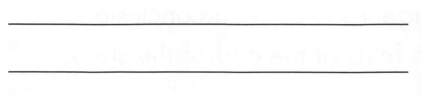

gift

visit

Surprising Treasures Think about how Juan was surprised. Tell a partner about a time when you were surprised.

Talk About It Review the words on page 138. Tell or show a partner what each word means.

Produce Language Write about a time when you were surprised with something or someone you treasure. First draw a picture of the surprise. Complete the sentences. Then write in your Weekly Concept Journal.

_____ was a surprise.

I treasure it because _____.

What treasures can we create?

Sometimes we create things for other people. Those people can think of those things as treasures. One thing you can create for someone is a card.

Read the passage together.
Then circle the vocabulary words.

The Card

Pam's friend Ana was sick.

Pam wanted to (create) a card for her.

"That is a great idea," said Mom.

So Pam made a card.

She drew a picture on the card.

"I think Ana will love your card," said Mom.

Talk About It Complete
the sentence below.

Pam _____ .
*drew a picture, made
a card*

Your Turn Tell a partner whom you
would create a card for and why.

Draw Conclusions We use special words, such as *I think*, to tell what we think and why. We say *because* to tell why.

I think that the dad and daughter like plants **because** they are planting flowers.

Talk About It Look at the picture. Tell what you think and why.

I think that _____ because _____.

Your Turn Look at the picture. Tell what you think.

I think that _____ because _____.

Draw Conclusions When you read a story or look at pictures, you can figure out more about a character or story and tell why you think so.

The family in the picture is creating something. Draw a conclusion about what the family is creating.

· ·

Talk About It Tell your partner your conclusion about the picture above.

> I think that _____ because _____.

· ·

Your Turn Look at the picture below of a girl making a necklace. Draw a conclusion about it.

_____

_____

Adjectives Words that are used to describe people, places, or things are called **adjectives.** Colors are adjectives.

yellow lemon

blue ball

Talk About It Use a color word to tell about the apple.

The _____ apple is good.

Your Turn Think about your favorite toy. Then write a sentence telling what color it is.

My _____ toy is my favorite.

Think, Talk, and Write

pottery

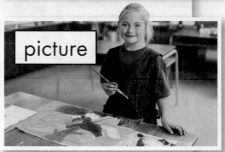

picture

Making Treasures Think about how Pam created a card for her friend Ana. Tell a partner about a treasure that you created or that someone else created for you.

Talk About It Review the words on page 144. Tell or show a partner what each word means.

Produce Language Write about a time when you created a treasure for someone. First draw a picture of what you made. Tell what it looked like. Complete the sentences. Then write in your Weekly Concept Journal.

I made a _____.

It was _____.

Vocabulary

PICTURE IT!

country

PICTURE IT!

flag

found
national
president
took

What treasures can we find in our country?

Our country is called the United States. There are many treasures we can find here. One of those treasures is the White House.

Read the passage together.
Then circle the vocabulary words.

The White House

My class (took) a trip to the White House.

The White House is in Washington, D.C.

The president of our country lives there.

The White House is a national treasure.

We also found out that the flag is a national treasure.

· ·

Talk About It Complete the sentence below.

> The White House is _____.
> *where the president lives,*
> *a national treasure*

· ·

Your Turn Tell a partner about the White House.

151

Describing When you write, you can use words to tell more about people, places, and things.

The flag is **big.**
It has **white** stars.

· ·

Talk About It Look at the picture.
Tell about the White House.

> The White House is _____.
>
> It has _____.

· ·

Your Turn Look at the picture.
Write a sentence that tells more
about the object.

The eagle is _____.

Details and Facts A **fact** is something that is true. **Details** tell more about a fact.

Fact: The president lives in the White House.

Detail: The president's office is called the Oval Office.

Talk About It Look at this picture. Tell your partner a fact about the statue.

The statue is _____ .

Your Turn Tell a fact or detail about the White House.

The White House is _____ .

Adjectives for Size Some words tell about the size of people, places, or things. These words tell how big or small things are.

big house   **little** house

tall flag   **short** flag

Talk About It Tell a partner about the size of the building.

It is a _____ building.

Your Turn Draw a picture of a treasure. Tell about its size.

Lincoln Memorial

Statue of Liberty

Our Country's Treasures

The White House is one of our country's treasures. Tell a partner something you treasure in our country.

Talk About It Review the words on page 150. Tell or show a partner what each word means.

Produce Language Write about something you treasure in our country. First draw a picture of the national treasure. Complete the sentences. Then write in your Weekly Concept Journal.

One of our country's treasures
is _____.

I like it because _____.

Vocabulary

fireworks

moon

above

celebrate

Why do we treasure special days?

During the year, we celebrate special days. We often spend those special days with special people. One of those days is July 4th.

Read the passage together.
Then circle the vocabulary words.

July 4th

In 1776, the United States became a country.

People (celebrate) every July 4th.

At night, people watch fireworks!

The fireworks light up the sky above.

They are bright like the moon.

Talk About It Complete
the sentence below.

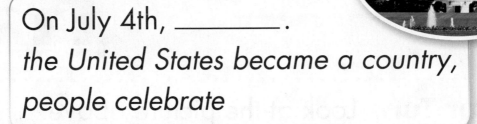

On July 4th, _____.
the United States became a country,
people celebrate

Your Turn Tell a partner about a day
you celebrate with your family.

Describing We use special words to tell about how people do things. Sometimes those words end in *-ly*.

The girls wave the flags **happily.**

The girls wave the flags **slowly.**

Talk About It Look at the picture. Tell a partner more about how the boy might be drumming.

The boy drums _____.

Your Turn Look at the picture above. Tell what the other boy is doing. Use a word that tells how.

_____

_____

Details and Facts A **fact** is something that is true. **Details** can tell more about a fact.

Fact: July 4th is the day the United States became a country.
Detail: We fly the flag on July 4th.

- -

Talk About It Tell your partner a fact about July 4th.

- -

Your Turn Tell a partner a fact about a day you celebrate. Then tell a detail about it.

Adjectives for What Kind Words that tell more about people, places, or things are called **adjectives.** They can answer the questions *What kind?* or *What colors?*

red, white, yellow, and **blue** fireworks

tasty food

Talk About It Look at this picture. Use words to answer the question *What colors?*

This is a _____ flag.

Your Turn Draw a picture of a celebration. Write a word to tell about the celebration.

The celebration is a

_____ celebration.

Think, Talk, and Write

Thanksgiving

New Year

Special Days The 4th of July is a special day that we treasure. Tell a partner about a special day that you and your family celebrate.

· ·

Talk About It Review the words on page 156. Tell or show a partner what each word means.

· ·

Produce Language Write about a special day that you and your family celebrate. First draw a picture of the special day. Complete the sentences. Then write in your Weekly Concept Journal.

A special day we celebrate is _____.

It is special because _____.

Vocabulary

family room

picture

**brought
miss**

What treasures can we share at home?

We all have things that are treasures. Some treasures can be found in our homes. One of those treasures can be a picture of someone in our family.

Read the passage together.
Then circle the vocabulary words.

The Picture

Laura sat in her (family room).

"I miss Grandpa," she said.

Grandpa's visit had been fun.

"I have an idea," said Mom.

Mom brought Laura a picture.

The picture was of Grandpa.

"Thank you!" said Laura.

Talk About It Complete the
sentence below.

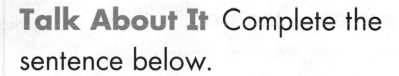

Mom _____.
had an idea, brought Laura a picture

Your Turn Tell a partner
about a treasure you have.

Retelling We use special words to tell about things that happened in the past. Some of these words end in *-ed*.

Laura **was** sad.
Laura **missed** her grandpa.
Mom **gave** Laura a picture.
Laura **smiled.**

Talk About It Tell your partner about a treasure you have at home.

> The treasure was _____.
>
> _____ gave me the treasure.

Your Turn Tell about a story you know. Use an *-ed* word.

In the story, _____.

Then, _____.

Character, Setting, Plot A **character** is a person or an animal in a story. The **setting** is where the story happens. The **plot** is what happens in the story.

Characters: Laura, Mom

Setting: family room of a house

Plot: First, Laura was sad because she missed her grandpa. Then, Mom brought Laura a picture. Finally, Laura was happy.

Talk About It Tell a partner about a story you know.

The characters are _____.

The setting is _____.

Your Turn Tell the plot of your story. Draw a picture or write a sentence.

Adjectives for How Many Words that are used to tell more about people, places, or things are called **adjectives.** Sometimes they can answer the question *How many?*

many pictures   **few** pictures   **one** picture

Talk About It Use a word to answer the question *How many pictures?*

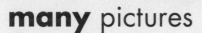 pictures

Your Turn Draw a picture showing few or many of something. Then write the word *few* or *many* below your picture.

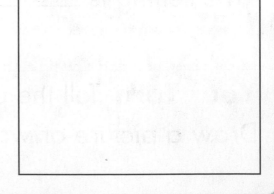

Treasures at Home Pictures can be special treasures that remind us of people we love. Tell a partner about a special treasure that you have at home.

old treasure

new treasure

Talk About It Review the words on page 162. Tell or show a partner what each word means.

Produce Language Write about a special treasure that you have at home. First draw a picture of your special thing. Complete the sentences. Then write in your Weekly Concept Journal.

A special treasure I have is _____.

It is special because _____.

garden

gate

because

neighbors

What treasures can we share with neighbors?

We all have treasures that we think are special. Some treasures, such as things from a garden, can be shared with our neighbors.

Read the passage together.
Then circle the vocabulary words.

The Garden

Alex and his dad opened the (garden) gate.

"Our tomatoes really grew!" said Dad.

"We should give some to our neighbors

because we have so many," said Alex.

"That's a good idea," said Dad.

· ·

Talk About It Complete the
sentence below.

> Alex and his dad _____.
> *grew tomatoes, shared
> tomatoes with their neighbors*

· ·

Your Turn Tell a partner about
a treasure you'd like to share
with a neighbor.

Cause-and-Effect Relationship We use special words to tell why things happen. Words such as *because* help us tell why things happen.

I gave some strawberries to my neighbors **because** I had so many.

The tomatoes are wet **because** I watered them.

Talk About It Look at the picture. Tell why something happened. Use the word *because*.

I picked the vegetables because _____.

Your Turn Tell about something you shared with a neighbor. Tell why you shared it.

I shared _____ with my neighbor because _____.

Cause and Effect Things we read tell causes and effects. A **cause** is why something happens. An **effect** is what happens. The word *because* shows that there is a cause.

The neighbor is happy **because** Luis gave her a picture.

· ·

Talk About It Look at the picture above. Read the sentence. What is the effect? What is the cause?

> The effect is _____.
>
> The cause is _____.

· ·

Your Turn Look at the story "The Garden" on page 169. What caused Alex and his dad to give their neighbors tomatoes?

Adjectives That Compare

Adjectives tell about people, places, or things. Sometimes they compare two things.

The first plant is **small.**   The second plant is **smaller.**

Talk About It Look at these pictures. Compare the two gardens.

The first garden is _____ than the second garden.

Your Turn Draw a picture of two carrots. One carrot is big. The other carrot is bigger.

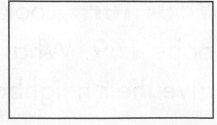

Think, Talk, and Write

Sharing Treasures Think about how Alex shared with his neighbors. Tell a partner about a special treasure that you could share with neighbors.

flowers

treats

Talk About It Review the words on page 168. Tell or show a partner what each word means.

Produce Language Write about a special treasure that you could share with a neighbor. First draw a picture. Complete the sentences. Then write in your Weekly Concept Journal.

A special treasure I could share is _____.

It is special because _____.

Get Online!

Hear it!
See it!
Do it!

- Big Question Video
- Concept Talk Video
- Envision It! Animation
- Grammar Jammer
- Daily Journal

Clever Solutions

THE BIG ? What difference can a great idea make?

Solving Problems
When does a problem need a clever solution?

New Ways to Do Things
How can we look at things in a different way?

Solving Mysteries
How do we solve mysteries?

Ideas That Make Life Easier
How can a great idea make our lives easier?

Ideas That Change Lives
How can a great idea change the way we live?

New Ideas
What can happen when someone has a new idea?

Clever Solutions

Vocabulary

PICTURE IT!

statue

PICTURE IT!

wagon

clever
how
pulled
solution
toward

When does a problem need a clever solution?

Sometimes a problem is hard to fix. We need to think about it for a long time. Then we find a solution that works.

Vocabulary in Context

Read the passage together.
Then circle the vocabulary words.

Clever Carla

(How) would Carla get her statue to school?

It was too big to carry.

Carla could use a big wagon.

It was a clever solution to her problem.

Carla pulled the statue toward her school.

Talk About It Complete the
sentences below.

Carla _____.
thinks of a clever solution, uses a wagon

_____ is big.
The statue, The wagon

Your Turn What is Carla's clever
solution? Tell a partner.

Comparing and Contrasting We use words to tell how things are alike and different. Words such as *big* and *small* tell size.

The wagon is **big.**

The statue is **big.**

Talk About It These statues are different. Complete the sentences.

> One statue is _____ .
>
> The other statue is _____ .

Your Turn Find a big thing and a small thing. Complete the sentences.

The _____ is big.

The _____ is small.

Compare and Contrast We **compare** when we tell how things are alike. We **contrast** when we tell how things are different.

Compare: The wagon is big. The statue is big.

Contrast: The wagon is red. The statue is gray.

Talk About It How are the pencil and crayon alike? Tell a partner.

The pencil _____. The crayon _____.

Your Turn Tell how the pencil and crayon are different.

The pencil is _____. The crayon is _____.

Commands We use **commands** to tell people to do things. Commands are sentences that end with a period.

Pull the wagon. — period

Solve the problem. — period

Talk About It Circle the command. Do what it says.

Touch your nose.

The wagon is big.

Your Turn Put a period at the end of each sentence. Circle the commands.

Tell a story

Carla pulled the wagon

Solve the problem

Think, Talk, and Write

Solving Problems Think about how Carla solved her problem. Tell a partner about a time when you solved a problem.

What is a solution?

. . . .

Talk About It Review the words on page 176. Tell or show a partner what each word means.

. . . .

Produce Language Write about a time when you solved a problem. First draw a picture of how you solved the problem. Complete the sentences. Then write in your Weekly Concept Journal.

A problem I had was _____.

So I _____.

New Ways to Do Things

Vocabulary

airplane

clouds

flew
should
turned
upside down

How can we look at things in a different way?

Sometimes our solutions do not work. We should try to look at the problem in a new way. Then we can think of a better solution.

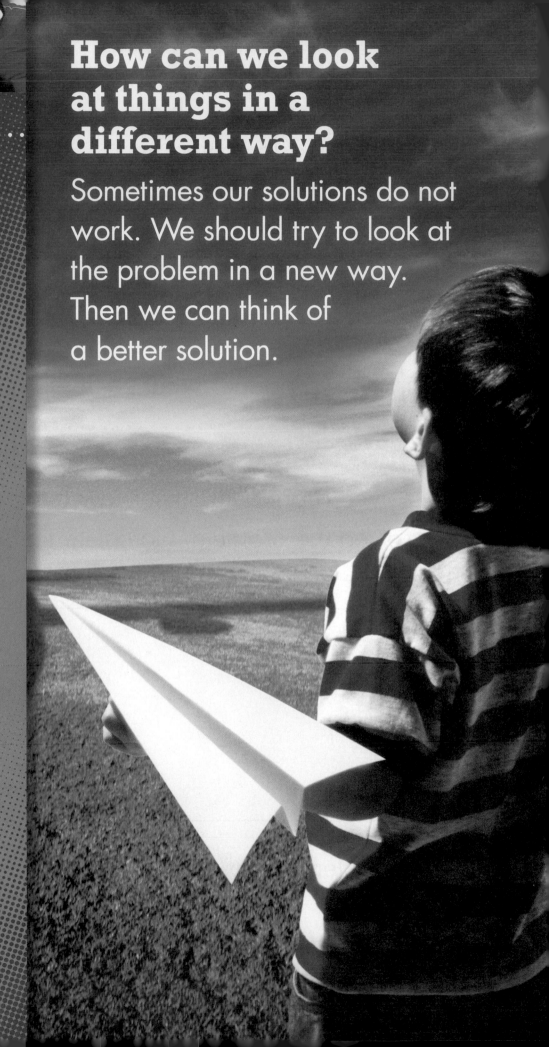

Read the passage together.
Then circle the vocabulary words.

Upside Down

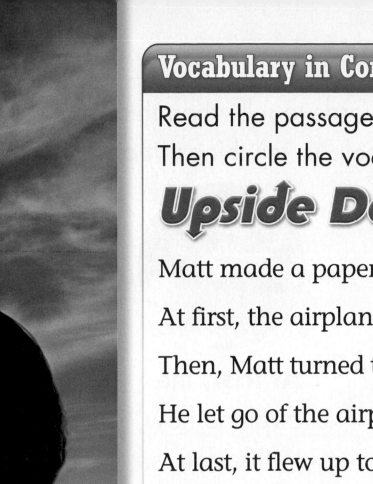

Matt made a paper (airplane).

At first, the airplane flew to the ground.

Then, Matt turned the airplane upside down.

He let go of the airplane.

At last, it flew up to the clouds!

· ·

Talk About It Complete the sentence below.

> Matt _____.
>
> *made a paper airplane, turned the airplane upside down, let go of the airplane*

· ·

Your Turn How did Matt look at the airplane in a different way? Tell a partner.

Sequencing We use words to tell when things happen. Special words help us tell things in order.

At first, the airplane fell to the ground.

At last, the airplane flew to the clouds.

Talk About It Circle the words that show order.

At first, the girl is sad.

At last, the girl is happy.

Your Turn Write *1* next to what happens first. Write *2* next to what happens last.

____ At last, I put on shoes.

____ At first, I put on socks.

Sequence **Sequence** is another word for order. When you read, look for words that tell order.

Order	What Happened
1	Matt made a paper airplane.
2	At first, the airplane would not fly up.
3	At last, Matt fixed the problem.

Talk About It These pictures are about fitting a table through a door. Tell the order of the pictures.

____   ____   ____

Your Turn Write *1*, *2*, and *3* to show the order.

____ Matt made a paper airplane.

____ At last, Matt fixed the problem.

____ At first, the airplane would not fly up.

Exclamations We use **exclamations** to show we are excited. Exclamations are sentences that end with an exclamation mark.

Anita solved the problem**!**   That airplane is big**!**

Talk About It Circle the exclamations.

Wow!

Matt turned the airplane upside down.

The airplane flew!

Your Turn Put an exclamation mark at the end of each sentence.

I love airplanes

I made an airplane too

Think, Talk, and Write

New Ways to Do Things

Think about how Matt solved his problem. Tell a partner about a time when you were able to come up with a better solution to a problem.

Try to see it a new way.

Talk About It Review the vocabulary on page 182. Tell or show a partner what each word means.

Produce Language Write about a time when you saw something in a new way. First draw a picture of how you solved the problem. Complete the sentences. Then write in your Weekly Concept Journal.

First I tried _____.

My better solution was _____.

PICTURE IT!

book

PICTURE IT!

closet

among
clues
looked
mystery
solve

How do we solve mysteries?

Some people need to find things that are lost. Some people need to know how something happened. These people look for clues to help them.

Read the passage together.
Then circle the vocabulary words.

Book Mystery

Where was Ian's book?

Ian wanted to solve this mystery.

Ian looked for clues.

Ian looked under his bed.

Ian looked among his toys.

Later Ian found the book in his closet!

Talk About It Complete the sentence below.

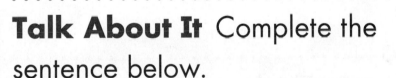

The book was _____.
missing, in the closet

Your Turn How did Ian solve the mystery? Tell a partner.

Explaining We use words to tell what people do.

Ty **looked** for his shoe.

Martina **found** her socks.

Talk About It Think of something you have looked for. Complete the sentence.

I looked for _____.

Your Turn What is something you have found? Tell a partner.

Main Idea and Details A **main idea** is the most important idea. **Details** tell about the main idea.

Main Idea	Details
The person is solving a mystery.	The person wears a tan coat. The person wears a hat.

Talk About It
Circle the main idea of "Book Mystery."

Ian likes books.

Ian wanted to find his book.

Ian's closet is messy.

Your Turn Write a detail from "Book Mystery."

_____

_____

191

How Sentences Begin and End All sentences begin with a capital letter, such as *A*, *B*, or *C*. All sentences end with an ending mark.

(W)here is the book(?)

[capital letter]   [ending mark]

(T)he book is over here(.)

[capital letter]   [ending mark]

(I)t is a good book(!)

[capital letter]   [ending mark]

Talk About It Fix what is wrong with the sentences.

where is my shoe?

Ian found a clue

Your Turn Rewrite the sentence. Use a capital letter. Use an ending mark.

the boy solved the mystery

clues

places

Solving Mysteries Think about how Ian solved his book mystery. Tell a partner how to solve a mystery.

Talk About It Review the vocabulary on page 188. Tell or show a partner what each word means.

Produce Language Write about how to solve a mystery. First draw a picture of how you solved a mystery. Complete the sentences. Then write in your Weekly Concept Journal.

First look for _____.

Then put the clues together to solve the _____.

Vocabulary

bikes

horses

enjoy
gas
idea
oil
today

How can a great idea make our lives easier?

A great idea can help us do something faster. It can give us more time. A great idea can also help us do something better.

Read the passage together.
Then circle the vocabulary words.

Cars

Long ago there were no cars.

People walked, rode (horses), and rode bikes.

Today people enjoy having cars.

People put oil and gas in their cars.

Then they take their cars to many places!

Talk About It Complete
the sentence below.

Long ago people _____.
*walked, rode horses,
rode bikes*

Your Turn How do cars help us?
Tell a partner.

Describing We use words to tell where people, places, and things are. Special words help us show where.

above	The sky is **above** the bikes.
under	The street is **under** the bikes.
behind	The blue bike is **behind** the other bikes.

Talk About It Tell what is above, under, and behind you.

_____ is above me.

_____ is under me.

_____ is behind me.

Your Turn Look at this picture.

What is under the red car?

What is behind the red car?

196

Graphic Sources Pictures that give us information are **graphic sources.**

window — *door* — *wheels*

- -

Talk About It Complete the sentences. Use the graphic source above to help you.

The _____ is above the door.

The _____ are under the car.

- -

Your Turn Look at the graphic source above. Use *above* or *below* to complete the sentence.

The door is _____ the window.

Pronouns Sometimes we use **pronouns** to name people, places, and things.

he	**He** rides a bike.
she	**She** rides a horse.
it	**It** is a car.
we	**We** ride in the car.
you	**You** have a great idea.
they	**They** walk.

Talk About It Complete the sentences. Use pronouns from above.

_____ is a bike.

_____ walks.

Your Turn Write a sentence about a car.

It 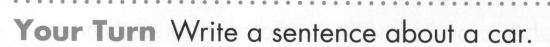 .

Think, Talk, and Write

Ideas That Make Life Easier

Think about how cars make our lives easier. Tell a partner how another great idea makes our lives easier.

phone

dishwasher

Talk About It Review the vocabulary on page 194. Tell or show a partner what each word means.

Produce Language

Write about a great idea that makes your life easier. First draw a picture of the thing. Complete the sentence. Then write in your Weekly Concept Journal.

_____ makes life easier

because _____ .

Ideas That Change Lives

Vocabulary

PICTURE IT!

letters

PICTURE IT!

phones

because
changed
learn
mail

How can a great idea change the way we live?

A great idea can help us do a thing we have never done before. This new thing can be helpful, fun, or both.

Read the passage together.
Then circle the vocabulary words.

Phones

Long ago people wrote (letters).

People waited for the mail.

Then phones changed people's lives.

Phones let people talk to each other.

Because of phones, people learn news faster.

. . . .

Talk About It Complete
the sentence below.

Phones _____.
*changed people's lives, let
people learn news faster*

. . . .

Your Turn Why are phones
a great idea? Tell a partner.

Asking Questions **Questions** are sentences that help us learn something. Questions end with a question mark.

Who is on
the phone**?**

What do you
want to say**?**

Talk About It Circle the question that can help you learn about the picture below.

Who wrote the letter?

Who is on the phone?

When will we eat?

Your Turn What question do you want to ask about the picture above? Tell a partner.

Draw Conclusions

We think about things
we read and see.
Then we make up our
minds about them.
This is how we
draw conclusions.

Conclusion: I think she is
finding out something good.

Talk About It Look at "Phones"
on page 201. Circle a conclusion.

Few people write letters now.

People like to find out things right away.

Phones are not a great idea.

Your Turn Draw a conclusion
about the picture. Tell a partner.

Pronouns *I* and *Me* We use *I* and *me* when we talk about ourselves. *I* usually comes at the start of a sentence. *Me* usually comes at the end of a sentence.

I	**I** am on the phone.
me	Someone is talking to **me.**

Talk About It Circle *I* and *me* in the sentences.

I like talking on the phone.

I want someone to call me.

Your Turn Complete the sentences. Use *I* or *me.*

Leslie sent a letter to _____.

_____ liked getting a letter!

Think, Talk, and Write

computers

airplanes

Ideas That Change Lives

Think about how phones have changed the way we live. Tell a partner how a great idea can change the way we live.

Talk About It Review the vocabulary on page 200. Tell or show a partner what each word means.

Produce Language Write about a great idea that has changed the way we live. First draw a picture of the thing. Complete the sentences. Then write in your Weekly Concept Journal.

_____ changed the way we live.

Now people can _____.

Vocabulary

robot

shoelaces

build
different
loose
retie
untie

What can happen when someone has a new idea?

A new idea is fun! A person might tell others about the idea. A person might make or build the idea for others to enjoy.

Read the passage together.
Then circle the vocabulary words.

Wendy's Robot

Wendy has a new and (different) idea.

Wendy will build a robot that ties shoelaces.

The robot will retie shoelaces that are loose.

The robot will untie shoelaces too.

Everyone will want this robot!

Talk About It Complete the sentences below.

Wendy _____.
has a new idea, wants to build a robot

The robot _____.
will retie shoelaces, will untie shoelaces

Your Turn Would you want Wendy's robot? Tell a partner why or why not.

Comparing We use words to tell how things are alike and different. Words that end in *-er* can help us.

The child is **bigger** than the robot.

The red shoes are **smaller** than the blue shoes.

Talk About It Circle the *-er* words below.

> The child is taller than the robot.
>
> The robot ties shoelaces faster than Wendy does.

Your Turn Complete the sentence. Use an *-er* word from above.

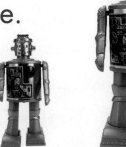

Robot A is _____ than Robot B.

Robot A   Robot B

Compare and Contrast When we tell how things are alike, we **compare.** When we tell how things are different, we **contrast.**

Compare	They are both robots.
Contrast	One robot is bigger than the other robot.

Talk About It Tell one way the robots above are alike. Tell one way the robots are different.

Your Turn How are the shoes alike? How are the shoes different? Tell a partner.

209

More About Pronouns Pronouns stand for people, places, and things. Pronouns often go at the ends of sentences.

him	Give a robot to **him.**
her	Give a robot to **her.**
it	Wendy will build **it.**
you	It will tie shoelaces for **you.**
us	It will also tie shoelaces for **us.**
them	We will get robots for **them.**

Talk About It Circle the pronouns below.

Wendy will build a robot for you.

Wendy will build it.

Your Turn Circle the correct pronoun.

Gus played with *(it, them).*

It does things for *(it, him).*

Think, Talk, and Write

New Ideas Think about how Wendy came up with a new and different idea. Tell a partner what can happen when a person has a new idea.

enjoy the idea

share the idea

Talk About It Review the vocabulary on page 206. Tell or show a partner what each word means.

Produce Language Write about a new idea that you have. First draw a picture of what you want to do or make. Complete the sentences. Then write in your Weekly Concept Journal.

I have a new _____.

My new idea is _____.

Glossary

How to Use This Glossary

This glossary can help you understand and pronounce some of the words in this book. The words at the top of each page show the first and last words on the page. The pronunciation key is on page 213. Remember, if you can't find the word you are looking for, ask for help or check a dictionary.

The entry word is in dark type. It shows how the word is spelled.

The pronunciation is in parentheses. It also shows which syllables are stressed.

Part-of-speech labels show the function of the word.

adapt (ə dapt′), *v.* to change your behavior or ideas to fit a new situation

Aa

above (ə buv′), *PREP.* in a higher place

again (ə gen′), *ADV.* one more time

airplane (âr′plān′), *N.* a vehicle that flies by using wings

always (ȯl′wāz), *ADV.* at all times

among (ə mung′), *PREP.* in a group of people or things

and (and), *CONJ.* a word used for joining two words, phrases, or parts of a sentence

Bb

be (bē), *v.* word used to describe people or things or give information about them

because (bi kȯz′), *CONJ.* used when you are giving the reason for something

bees (bēz), *N.* flying insects that make honey and can sting you

before (bi fôr′), *PREP.* earlier than

bicycle (bī′sik′əl), *N.* a vehicle with two wheels that you sit on and ride

bikes (bīks), *N.* more than one bicycle

birds (bėrdz), *N.* animals with wings and feathers that lay eggs and usually can fly

bloom (blüm), *v.* to make flowers

boats (bōts), *N.* small ships that float in the water

book (bů k), *N.* a set of printed pages held together in a cover so you can read them

branches (branch′iz), *N.* parts of a tree that grow out from the middle

brought (brȯt), *v.* carried or arrived at a new place

build (bild), *v.* to make something by putting pieces together

building (bild′ing), *N.* something with a roof and walls such as a house, office, or school

Cc

card (kärd), N. a piece of stiff paper with a picture on the front and a message inside

cat (kat), N. a small, furry animal that people often keep as a pet

celebrate (sel′ə brāt), v. to have a special meal or party because something good has happened

chain (chān), N. a group of things joined together

changed (chānjd), v. made something different or became different

clean (klēn), ADJ. not dirty

clever (klev′ər), ADJ. showing ability or skill, especially at making things or doing things

closet (kloz′it), N. a tall cupboard built into the wall of a room, used to store things

clouds (kloudz), N. white or gray masses in the sky, from which rain falls

cloudy (kloud′ē), ADJ. having a dark sky, full of clouds

clues (klüz), N. things that help you find the answer to a difficult problem

come (kum), v. to move toward someone or something

communities (kə myü′nə tēz), N. places where people live

continue (kən tin′yü), v. to keep happening or do something without stopping

country (kun′trē), N. a nation with its land and people

create (krē āt′), v. to make something new

Dd

different (dif′ər ənt), ADJ. not the same

dolphins (dol′fənz), N. gray sea animals with long pointed noses

drank (drangk), v. swallowed liquid

drew (drü), v. made lines on paper or some other surface

drops (drops), N. small amounts of liquid

a in hat	ėr in term	ô in order	ch in child	ə = a in about
ā in age	i in it	oi in oil	ng in long	ə = e in taken
â in care	ī in ice	ou in out	sh in she	ə = i in pencil
ä in far	o in hot	u in cup	th in thin	ə = o in lemon
e in let	ō in open	u̇ in put	ŦH in then	ə = u in circus
ē in equal	ȯ in all	ü in rule	zh in measure	

Ee

eggs (egz), N. round objects with hard shells that contain a baby bird, snake, fish, or insect

elephant (el'ə fənt), N. a very large, gray animal with big ears and a long nose called a trunk

enjoy (en joi'), V. to get pleasure and happiness from something

every (ev'rē), ADJ. each one

examined (eg zam'ənd), V. looked at someone or something closely and carefully

Ff

family (fam'ə lē), N. a group of people who are related to each other, especially a father, mother, and their children

family room (fam'ə lē rüm), N. a room in a house where a family spends time together

fireworks (fīr'wėrks'), N. explosives that make a lot of bright light and color in the air

fixed (fikst), V. repaired something

flag (flag), N. a piece of cloth with a special pattern on it, used as the symbol of a country or organization

flew (flü), V. moved through the air or wind

flying (flī'ing), V. moving through the air

follow (fol'ō), V. to come or go after someone or something

food (füd), N. what you eat

found (found), V. came upon someone or something

friends (frendz), N. people whom you like and trust very much

Gg

garden (gärd'n), N. a piece of land where flowers or vegetables are grown

gas (gas), N. a liquid that makes cars and trucks move

gate (gāt), N. the part of a wall or fence that you can open like a door

gather (gaŦH'ər), V. to come together in a group

geese (gēs), N. birds with long necks that are related to ducks

good (gud), ADJ. enjoyable and pleasant

grandson (grand'sun'), N. the son of your son or daughter

grass (gras), N. a common plant with thin, green leaves that covers land

great (grāt), ADJ. very good

ground (ground), N. the surface of the earth

Hh

help (help), *v.* to do something for someone

herd (hėrd), *N.* a group of animals of the same kind

hiker (hīk′ər), *N.* someone who takes a long walk in the country or in the mountains

hive (hīv), *N.* a place where bees live

hole (hōl), *N.* an empty space or opening in something

horses (hôrs′ez), *N.* large animals that people ride on and use for pulling heavy things

house (hous), *N.* a building that you live in, especially with your family

how (hou), *ADV.* used for asking about something or explaining how you do things

Ii

idea (ī dē′ə), *N.* a thought or plan that you think of

insects (in′sektz), *N.* bugs that have six legs, such as flies

inside (in′sīd), *N.* the inner part of something

Jj

janitor (jan′ə tər), *N.* someone who cleans a building and repairs things in it

Kk

kitten (kit′n), *N.* a young cat

Ll

land (land), *N.* ground or surface of the earth

leads (lēdz), *v.* brings others in a specific direction

learn (lėrn), *v.* to get knowledge of something or the ability to do something

letters (let′ərz), *N.* written messages that you put into an envelope and send to someone by mail

litter (lit′ər), *N.* waste paper and other trash that people leave on the ground in public

looked (lu̇kd), *v.* saw something with your eyes

loose (lüs), *ADJ.* not firmly attached to something

lost (lȯst), *ADJ.* unable to find the way

Mm

mail (māl), *N.* the letters and packages that are delivered to a place

make (māk), *v.* to create something or put something together

many (men′ē), *ADJ.* a lot; a large number of

meal (mēl), N. the food that you eat at one time

medicine (med′ə sən), N. a substance given to help sick people get better

meerkats (mir′kats), N. small African animals that have grey coats, stand near their homes, and live in groups

migrate (mī′grāt), V. to move from one place to another to live or find work

miss (mis), V. to feel sad when someone is not there

moon (mün), N. the large, round object that shines in the sky at night

my (mī), ADJ. belonging to the person speaking

mystery (mis′tər ē), N. something that is difficult to explain or understand

Nn

national (nash′ə nəl), ADJ. relating to a country

neighbors (nā′bərz), N. people who live near you

nest (nest), N. a place made by a bird, insect, or small animal to live in

nice (nīs), ADJ. pleasant, good, or attractive

nurse (nėrs), N. someone who is trained to take care of people who are sick or injured

Oo

ocean (ō′shən), N. a very large area of water

oil (oil), N. thick, dark liquid that makes machines work smoothly

our (our), ADJ. belonging to us

Pp

people (pē′pəl), N. more than one person

pet (pet), N. an animal that you take care of and keep at your house

phones (fōnz), N. objects that you use to speak to someone in another place

picture (pik′chər), N. a drawing, painting, or photograph

playground (plā′ground′), N. a small area of land where children play

president (prez′ə dənt), N. the official leader of a country

principal (prin′sə pəl), N. someone who is in charge of a school

protect (prə tekt′), V. to prevent someone or something from being harmed or damaged

pulled (pùld), *v.* moved something or someone toward yourself

push (pùsh), *v.* to move with a force

Qq

queen (kwēn), *N.* the female ruler of a country or other area

Rr

rain (rān), *N.* drops of water that fall from the sky

rescue (res′kyü), *v.* to save someone from danger

retie (rē tī′), *v.* to fasten things with a rope or string again

return (ri tėrn′), *v.* to come back or go back to a place

riding (rīd′ing), *v.* being carried on an animal or on a bicycle

robot (rō′bot), *N.* a machine that moves and works instead of a person

Ss

safe (sāf), *ADJ.* not in danger of being harmed or destroyed

scared (skâr′d), *v.* made someone feel afraid

scent (sent), *N.* the smell left behind by a person or animal

school (skül), *N.* a place where children go to learn

scientists (sī′ən tists), *N.* people who work in science

sea turtle (sē tėr′tl), *N.* an animal with a hard shell over its body that lives mainly in the water

shoelaces (shü′lās′es), *N.* long pieces of string that are used to make shoes fit tightly on your feet

should (shùd), *v.* a helping verb used when saying what is expected

sick (sik), *ADJ.* not healthy; having a disease

slept (slept), *v.* rested with eyes closed

soccer (sok′ər), *N.* a game in which two teams of eleven players try to kick a ball between two posts at either end of a field

solution (sə lü′shən), *N.* a way of solving a problem or dealing with a difficult situation

solve (solv), *v.* to find the answer to something

some (sum), *ADJ.* an amount or number of something

soon (sün), *ADV.* in a short time from now

south (south), *N.* the direction that is opposite of north

Glossary

217

spring (spring), N. the season between winter and summer, when plants start to grow again

stands (standz), v. is upright in a certain place

statue (stach′ü), N. a shape of a person or animal made of stone, metal, or wood

strong (strȯng), ADJ. having a lot of power or force

study (stud′ē), v. to learn about a subject

sure (shur), ADJ. certain about something

surprise (sər prīz′), N. something that is not expected or usual

Tt

take (tāk), v. to bring from one place to another

these (ᴛнēz), ADJ. the ones here; the ones nearer than that one

things (thingz), N. objects

think (thingk), v. to use your mind to decide something, have ideas, or solve problems

this (ᴛнis), ADJ. the one here; the one nearer than that one

today (tə dā′), N. the present time

took (tuk), v. led or carried along to another place

torn (tôrn), v. pulled apart by force

toward (tôrd), PREP. in the direction of

treasure (trezh′ər), N. someone or something with a lot of value

tree (trē), N. a large plant with branches, leaves, and a thick trunk

turned (ternd), v. moved so that you are looking in a new direction

Uu

under (un′dər), PREP. in or to a lower place that is below something

untie (un tī′), v. to take apart a knot or something that is tied

upside down (up′sīd′ doun′), ADV. in a position with the top at the bottom and the bottom on top

use (yüz), v. to put into action

Vv

value (val′yü), N. the amount of importance that something has

vet (vet), N. an animal doctor; short for veterinarian

Ww

wagon (wag′ən), N. a vehicle with four wheels that can be pulled

wait (wāt), v. to stay in place until something happens

want (wänt), *v.* to have a desire or need for something

wash (wäsh), *v.* to make something clean using water and soap

weather (weŦH′ər), *N.* the temperature and conditions such as wind, rain, or sun

whales (wālz), *N.* very large animals that live in the ocean and breathe through a hole in the top of their heads

wheels (wēlz), *N.* the round things under a vehicle that turn around and around and allow it to move

won't (wōnt), *v.* will not

woods (wu̇dz), *N.* a small forest

would (wu̇d), *v.* a helping verb used to say a want or desire

Credits

Illustrations
2 Joe LeMonnier; 4 Rick Drennan; 5 Shennen Bersani; 5 Kathy McCord; 5 Erica Pelton Vilnave

Photographs
Every effort has been made to secure permission and provide appropriate credit for photographic material. The publisher deeply regrets any omission and pledges to correct errors called to its attention in subsequent editions.

Unless otherwise acknowledged, all photographs are the property of Pearson Education, Inc.

Photo locators denoted as follows: Top (T), Center (C), Bottom (B), Left (L), Right (R), Background (Bkgd)

6 (TL) ©Greg Wright/Alamy, (BL) ©Cydney Conger/Corbis, (C) Redcover.com/Getty Images, ©Abode/Beateworks/ Corbis, ©Jose Luis Pelaez, Inc./Corbis, ©Jon Feingersh/Masterfile Corporation, ©Masterfile Royalty-Free, ©David Grossman/Alamy Images; 8 (TL) Julia Fishkin/Jupiter Images, (TC) Ryan McVay/Getty Images, (CR) Jupiterimages/ Jupiter Images, (BR) Diana Koenigsberg/Jupiter Images; 9 (TR) ©PhotoAlto/Alamy; 10 (TL) Andy Crawford and Gary Ombler/©DK Images, (CR) Steve Shott/©DK Images, (CL) ©Jupiterimages/BananaStock/Alamy, (CR) Lilly Dong/Jupiter Images; 11 (TC) Elizabeth Whiting & Associates/Corbis; 12 (TL) Jupiter Images, (CL) Getty Images, (C) Zia Solell/Getty Images, (BL) Lilly Dong/Jupiter Images; 14 (TL) Jupiter Images, (TC) Ken Hayden/Getty Images, (TR) ©Design Pics Inc./Alamy; 15 (TR) Getty Images, (BL) ©Corbis Premium RF/Alamy, (BR) ©Jupiterimages/Creatas/Alamy, (BC) ©Jupiterimages/Comstock Images/Alamy; 16 (TL) ©Jupiterimages/Creatas/Alamy, (CL) ©Glow Images/Alamy, (TC) ImageShop/Jupiter Images, (TR) ©Jupiterimages/Creatas/Alamy; 17 (TR) Megan Maloy/Getty Images; 18 (TL) Cyril Laubscher/©DK Images, (CL) Neil Fletcher/©DK Images; (C) Lillian Elaine Wilson/Jupiter Images; 19 (CR) Cyril Laubscher/©DK Images; 21 (TL) Getty Images, (TR) ©Jupiterimages/Polka Dot/Alamy, (TC) Ron Evans/Getty Images; 22 (TL) Jupiter Images, (TC) Getty Images, (TR) Nancy Brown/Getty Images, (CL) LWA/Getty Images, (CC) Sami Sarkis/ Getty Images, (CR) DCA Productions/Getty Images, (BR) Getty Images; 24 (TL) ©DLILLC/Corbis, (CL) Petra Wegner/ Alamy Images, (BL) Getty Images, (C) GK Hart/Vikki Hart, (TL) Frank Siteman/Stock Boston, Kaz Chiba/Getty Images, (TL) © Royalty-Free/Corbis, (TL) ©Mast Irham/epa/Corbis, (TL) Dennis Avon/Ardea.com, (TL) Jupiter Images, (CL) ©Comstock Inc., (C) Pixtal/Punchstock; 25 (TR) Tracy Morgan/©DK Images; 26 (TL) ©UpperCut Images/Alamy, (TR) Constance Bannister/Jupiter Images, (BR) H. Armstrong Roberts/Corbis, (TL) Blue Lantern Studio/Corbis, (TR) ©Jupiterimages/Creatas/Alamy, (BR) ©Blend Images/Alamy; 27 (TR) Getty Images, (CR) Ed Kashi/Corbis; 28 (CL) ©David Cook/blueshiftstudios/Alamy, (BR) Torahiko Yamashita, (TR) Bread and Butter/Getty Images; 29 (TR) Altrendo Images/Getty Images, (C) Getty Images; 30 (TL) Juniors Bildarchiv/Alamy Images, (CL) Rob Meinychuk/Getty Images, (BL) Ariel Skelley, (C) Steve Lynne/©DK Images, (TL) Getty Images, (CL) Getty Images, (BL) Getty Images, (C) Jose Luis Pelaez/Getty Images; 31 (TR) ©DK Images; 32 (TL) Pat Doyle/Corbis, (TR) IPS Co., LTD/Beateworks/Corbis, (BR) ©Juniors Bildarchiv/Alamy, (TC) ©Image Source , (TR) Lori Adamski-Peek/Jupiter Images, (BR) Jupiter Images; 33 (CL) ©Jupiterimages/Comstock Images/Alamy, (CR) ©Corbis Premium RF/Alamy; 34 (TL) Olaf Doering/Alamy Images, (C) Jeremy Woodhouse/Masterfile Corporation, (CR) GK Hart/Vikki Hart/Taxi, (BL) Dale C. Spartas/Corbis, (BR) GK Hart/ Vikki Hart/Stone, (TR) ©Corbis Premium RF/Alamy, (CC) ©Michael Newman/PhotoEdit, (CR) ©DK Images, (BC) ©Daniel Hurst/Acclaim Images, (BR) Getty Images, (B) ©Michael Newman/PhotoEdit; 35 (TR) Jupiter Images, (TR) Guy Call - The Stock Connection/Getty Images; 36 (CL) ©Jupiterimages/Creatas/Alamy, (TL) Brad Wrobleski, (C) ©Jupiterimages/Thinkstock/Alamy, (TL) Getty Images, (CL) ©Purestock/Alamy, (C) Jupiter Images, (CL) ©Jupiterimages/Creatas/Alamy; 37 (TR) ©Jupiterimages/Thinkstock/Alamy, (CR) ©Image Source ; 38 (TL) Tom Bear/ Aurora Photos, (TR) ©Marmaduke St. John/Alamy, (BR) Robert Percy/Animals Animals/Earth Scenes, (TL) Blend Images/Jupiter Images, (TC) Rolf Bruderer/Corbis, (TR) Stephen Weistead/Corbis, (BL) ©Jupiterimages/BananaStock/ Alamy; 39 (TR) ©Jupiterimages/Thinkstock/Alamy;,(TR) Bob Krist/Corbis, (BR) HIII Creek Pictures, (TL) Getty Images, (TC) Corbis/Jupiter Images; 41 (TR) Andrew Leyerle/Getty Images, Altrendo Images/Getty Images; 42 (TL) ©Kitt Cooper-Smith/Alamy, (CL) Steve Bloom, (BL) Michael Patrick O'Neil/Alamy Images, (C) Gerard Lacz/Animals Animals/ Earth Scenes; 43 (TR) ©SBI/NASA/Getty Images; 44 (BR) Gerard Lacz/Animals Animals/Earth Scenes; 45 (TR) Tasmanian Parks and Wildlife Service, Liz Wren, HO/AP Images, (BR) Corbis/Jupiter Images; 46 (TR) Joseph Van Os; 48 (TL) Mark Chappell/Animals Animals/Earth Scenes, (C) M. Truchon/Fotolia; 49 (CR) Martin Shields/Alamy Images; 50 (TR) Andrew Parkinson/Corbis, (CR) Steve Byland/Fotolia; 51 (TR) Andrew Paterson/Alamy Images; 52 (TR) Papilio/ Alamy Images, (BR) ©age fotostock/SuperStock; 53 (C) Getty Images; 54 (TL) M. Colbeck/OSF/Animals Animals/Earth Scenes, (CL) Stan Osolinski, (C) Paul Souders/Corbis; 55 (TR) George Diebold/Getty Images; 56 (TL) Markus Botzek/ zefa/Corbis, (TR) blickwinkel/Alamy Images, (TL) blickwinkel/Alamy Images; 57 (TR) Volkmar K. Wentzel/National

Geographic/Getty Images, (BR) Aroc Images/Alamy Images; 58 (TR) Peter Johnson/Corbis, (CR) Digital Vision, (BR) M. Colbeck/OSF/Animals Animals/Earth Scenes; 59 (C) Steve & Ann Toon/Getty Images; 60 (TL) Ariel Skelley/Corbis, (TL) © Patrick Ward/Corbis, © Stephen Frink/Corbis; 61 (TL) Masterfile Corporation, © Stephen Frink/Corbis, (TL) ©David Aubrey/Photo Researchers, Inc., Tim Laman/NGS Image Collection; 62 (TL) Getty Images, (CL) Jacek Chabraszewski/Fotolia, (C) Radius Images/Jupiter Images; 63 (CR) ©Jupiterimages/Brand X/Alamy, (CR) ©Jupiterimages/Brand X/Alamy; 64 (TR) Ariel Skelley/Corbis, (TR) Tom Stewart/Corbis, (BR) FoodPix/Jupiter Images; 65 (BR) Getty Images, (TR) Jose Luis Pelaez, Inc./Corbis; 66 (TR) Getty Images, (CR) Somos/Punchstock, (CR) ©DK Images, (BR) Corbis; 67 Ariel Skelley/Getty Images, (TR) Jenny Acheson/Getty Images; 68 (CL) ©Blend Images/Alamy, (C) Getty Images, (TL) Muntz/Taxi/Getty Images; 69 (TR) ©Jupiterimages/Comstock Images/Alamy; 70 (TR) Getty Images, (BR) Alvis Upitis/SuperStock; 71 (TR) ©Ron Chapple Stock/Corbis, (CR) Dave Nagel/Stone/Getty Images, (BR) Getty Images; 72 (TL) ©Jupiterimages/Creatas/Alamy, (TC) Getty Images, (TR) Todd Gipstein/National Geographic/Getty Images, (CR) Kim Sayer/©DK Images, (BR) Siri Stafford/Riser/Getty Images, (BR) Cooperphoto/Corbis; 73 (C) Jupiter Images, Elyse Lewin/Getty Images; 74 (TL) Andy Crawford/©DK Images, (CL) ©Tom Grill/Corbis, (BL) Jupiter Images, (C) Ariel Skelley/Corbis; 75 (TR) ©DK Images; 76 (TR) ©Blend Images/Alamy, (BR) Getty Images; 77 (TR) ©Jupiterimages/Thinkstock/Alamy, (BR) Mitchell Funk/Photographer's Choice/Getty Images; 78 (TL) Brad Wilson/Stone/Getty Images, (TC) ©Jupiterimages/Comstock Images/Alamy, (TR) Getty Images, (C) ©Jupiterimages/Creatas/Alamy, (C) ©UpperCut Images/Alamy, (C) Getty Images; 79 (TR) ©Elfi Kluck/Index Stock Imagery; 80 (TL) image100/Jupiter Images, (CL) David MacDonald/Oxford Scientific Films,Ltd./PhotoLibrary Group Ltd., Gallo Images ROOTS RF collection/Getty Images, (C) ©Peter Lilja/Jupiter Images; 81 (TR) Dorling Kindersley/Getty Images, Getty Images; 82 ©Royalty-Free/Corbis, ©Corbis Premium RF/Alamy, Corbis/Jupiter Images; 83 (TL) David MacDonald/Oxford Scientific Films,Ltd./PhotoLibrary Group Ltd., (TC) Winfried Wisniewski/Getty Images, (TR) David MacDonald/Oxford Scientific Films,Ltd./PhotoLibrary Group Ltd., (BL) Steve Bronstein/Getty Images, Getty Images, (BC) Steve Bronstein/Getty Images; 85 (TR) Doug Allan/Getty Images, (CR) David Davis/Fotolia; 86 (TL) Getty Images, (CL) ©Jupiterimages/Creatas/Alamy, (CL) ©Jupiterimages/Brand X/Alamy, (C) Getty Images; 87 (CR) ©Blend Images/Alamy; 88 (TL) ©PhotoAlto/Alamy, (TC) David Woodfall/Riser/Getty Images, (TR) Getty Images, (BR) John Foxx/Stockbyte/Getty Images, (BR) Ghislain & Marie David de Lossy/Iconica/Getty Images, (BR) Gordon Clayton/©DK Images; 90 ©Tony Cordoza/Alamy, (CR) smereka/Shutterstock; 91 (TR) Jeff Foott/Getty Images, Beverly Joubert/National Geographic Image Collection; 92 (TL) Grant Helman, (TL) ©Jupiterimages/Polka Dot/Alamy, (CL) Corbis/Jupiter Images, (CL) Getty Images, (C) Fotolia; 93 (TR) Getty Images, (BR) WILDLIFE GmbH/Alamy Images; 94 (TL) Frank Greenaway/Dorling Kindersley/Getty Images, (TC) Getty Images, (BC) Jerry Young/Dorling Kindersley/Getty Images, (BR) Paul Taylor/Stone/Getty Images; 95 (TR) Mitchell Funk/Getty Images, (BC) Geoff Dann/©DK Images, (BR) ©Jupiterimages/Creatas/Alamy, (TL) Bambuh/Fotolia; 96 (TL) Paulo De Oliveira/Oxford Scientific/Jupiter Images, (TR) Getty Images, (BR) MARIA STENZEL/National Geographic Image Collection; 97 (TR) Corbis/Jupiter Images, (CR) Getty Images; 98 ©Craig Tuttle/Corbis; 99 (TL) ©Visions of America, LLC/Alamy Images, (TL) © Jim Craigmyle/Corbis, (TL) ©Ariel Skelley/Corbis, (TL) ©Hans Strand/Corbis; 100 (TL) Jupiter Images, (CL) Raul Touzon/National Geographic Image Collection, (C) Construction Photography/Corbis; 101 (TR) Peter Daxeley/Photographer's Choice/Getty Images; 102 (TL) Getty Images, (TR) ©Look Photography/Beateworks/Corbis; 103 (TL) Malcom Fife/Photographer's Choice/Getty Images, (TR) Jupiter Images, (BL) Jack Fields/Corbis, (BR) Scott T. Smith/Corbis; 104 (TR) Comstock Images, (BR) ©Blend Images/Alamy; 105 Martin Ruegner/Getty Images, The Photolibrary Wales/Alamy Images; 106 (TL) Getty Images, (CL) image100/Jupiter Images, (C) Getty Images; 107 (CR) Getty Images; 108 (TL) Adamsmith/Taxi/Getty Images, (TR) ©Jupiterimages/BananaStock/Alamy; 110 (TR) Jupiter Images, (BR) Philip James Corwin/Corbis; 111 (C) National Geographic/Getty Images, (C) ©PhotoAlto/Alamy; 112 (TL) Jupiter Images, (CL) Getty Images, (BL) Imagemore/Getty Images, (C) Phoebe Dunn/Stock Connection/Jupiter Images; 113 (TR) ©DK Images; 114 (BR) ©Jupiterimages/Comstock Premium/Alamy; 115 (CL) Tim Ridley/©DK Images; 116 (TR) ©Jupiterimages/Brand X/Alamy, (BR) amana images/Getty Images; 117 (C) Getty Images, (C) ©Corbis Super RF/Alamy; 118 (CL) ©Corbis Premium RF/Alamy, (C) Timothy Shonnard/Workbook Stock/Jupiter Images; 119 (TR) Getty Images, (BR) image100/Jupiter Images; 120 (CL) ©PhotoAlto/Alamy, (C) Jupiter Images; 121 (C) amana images/Getty Images, (TR) Getty Images, (BR) Open Door Images/Jupiter Images; 122 (TR) ©Blend Images/Alamy, (CR) Getty Images; 123 (C) Brian Cosgrove/©DK Images, Adam Jones/Getty Images; 124 (TL) Clyde Laubscher/©DK Images, (CL) Luca Trovato/Botanica/Jupiter Images, (C) Harald Sund/Riser/Getty Images; 125 (TR) Rose Hodges/Food Pix/Jupiter Images; 126 (TL) Clyde Laubscher/©DK Images, (TR) Ethan Meleg/All Canada Photos/Getty Images, (CL) Jane Burton/Dorling Kindersley/Getty Images, (C) Yva Momatiuk/Corbis/Corbis, (CR) Dave